Journey

THROUGH THE NEW TESTAMENT

TIM CHRISTOSON

First published in 2019 by Striving Together Publications, a ministry of Lancaster Baptist Church, Lancaster, CA 93535. Striving Together Publications is committed to providing tried, trusted, and proven books that will further equip local churches to carry out the Great Commission. Your comments and suggestions are valued.

Striving Together Publications
4020 E. Lancaster Blvd.
Lancaster, CA 93535
800.201.7748

Cover and layout design by Andrew Jones
Edited by Monica Bass and Denise Lee

The contents of this book are the result of decades of spiritual growth in life and ministry. It is not our intent to claim originality with any quote or thought that could not readily be tied to an original source.

ISBN 978-1-59894-421-1

Printed in the United States of America

TO

FROM

· DEDICATION ·

TO MY CHILDREN

Taylor, McKinley, Grant, Monroe

It's a joy to be your dad! It thrills my heart to observe your desire to know and follow the Lord Jesus Christ. As you read and receive God's Word over the course of your lives, I pray that you will discover His love, receive His grace, embrace His truth, and become increasingly aware of His greatness, as we anticipate eternity in His glorious presence.

· CONTENTS ·

Table of Contents

· INTRODUCTION ·

WELCOME TO A NINETY-DAY JOURNEY THROUGH THE NEW TESTAMENT! Over the next three months, you will read through the entire New Testament, one day at a time.

As the very inspired Word of God, the Bible is not only captivating, but it is also *life changing*. I pray that as you read and meditate daily on the New Testament over these ninety days, you will come to better know your Saviour and experience His wisdom, love and guidance.

This devotional is designed to serve as your personal companion on a journey through your own copy of the New Testament.

Each daily devotion begins with a brief overview description of that day's Bible passage (given at the top of the page). Read this overview before reading the passage in your own Bible to gain a sense of the background and main themes of the passage.

The overview is followed by a devotional application from one portion of that day's reading. These were thoughts I recorded as I journeyed through the New Testament myself, along with friends and the church family where I pastor.

Each devotion concludes with a prayer, written from my perspective. Feel free to join me in that prayer or use it as a kickstart for your own prayer. I have also included one verse from the day's passage that you can meditate on and consider memorizing.

After each devotion, you can use the blank lines provided to journal your thoughts on the day's reading or write your own prayer.

Here are three tips to make the most of your ninety-day journey:

First, set an appointment with God. Decide what time each day you'll devote to this journey. Consider the following times:

- Right when you wake up (this works best for me…with coffee!)
- When the kids nap (for those with young children)
- Once the kids are off to school (for those with school-aged children)
- During your lunch break
- Right after dinner (instead of watching television)
- Just before bedtime (instead of social media)

Whatever time works for you, it's best if you can start each day's reading in a quiet spot where you have twenty–thirty undistracted minutes.

Second, whisper a brief prayer, asking God to speak to you. (Sometimes I pray the words of Psalm 119:18: "Open thou mine eyes, that I may behold wondrous things out of thy law.") As you read the Scripture, pay attention, visualize the scene, and be sensitive to phrases or principles that stand out to you. Remember, this is God's message to you, so expect it to be customized for you, by His Spirit.

Third, if you miss a day, don't sweat it. Just get back on track the following day. At some point, you can double-up, or you may take slightly more than ninety days to finish. If you miss a day occasionally, it won't ruin the journey. But if you stop completely, you'll miss out on what God wants to accomplish in your life through His Word.

May God bless you as you pursue Him!

Your friend,
Tim Christoson

90
DAY
DEVOTIONAL

Journey

THROUGH THE **NEW TESTAMENT**

DEVOTIONS

DAY 1

MATTHEW 1–4

The Long-Awaited Arrival of Jesus, His Baptism, and Victory over Temptation

OVERVIEW

The first four books of the New Testament (Matthew, Mark, Luke, and John) are separate biographies of the earthly life of Jesus. We call them *Gospels* because they contain the ultimate good news of Jesus Christ. While there is some repetition in the events the four writers recorded from Jesus' life, each of the four viewed His life from a different angle. And all of them wrote by the supernatural guidance of the Holy Spirit (2 Timothy 3:16, 2 Peter 1:21).

Matthew was one of only two apostles to write a Gospel (the other was John), and his record is unique in providing evidence to the Jews that Jesus is indeed the Messiah, the subject of centuries of prophecies. Don't get intimidated by the first seventeen verses, which contain the genealogy of Jesus from Joseph's side. (Luke contains the genealogy from Mary's side, and both are significant. Joseph was not Jesus' biological father, but his lineage traces back to David, making good on Old Testament prophecies concerning the Messiah. Mary's lineage also traces back to David, through another of his sons.) Once you get past this tough-to-pronounce-but-important family tree, it reads just like any story. And it's the greatest true story ever told: God became man to rescue mankind from the penalty of sin.

APPLICATION

Notice how many times Matthew writes something like, "that it might be fulfilled." You'll see it in the details surrounding Jesus' birth in 1:22, 2:15, 2:17, and 2:23. Matthew goes on to use this language repeatedly throughout his Gospel (8:17, 12:17, 13:35, 21:4, 26:54, etc.).

The point? God always keeps His promises. He is faithful. And He is able. I'm not. Sometimes I let my friends and family down because I forget or I get distracted. Other times, despite my best attempts, I am simply unable to carry out my good intentions. But God never fails. He never promises anything He isn't both able and willing to accomplish. No one and nothing will stand in His way—ever. When He promises to forgive you if you'll ask, He will (1 John 1:9). When He promises to provide for you if you'll seek Him first, He will (Matthew 6:33). When He promises to keep your salvation secure through the ups and downs of life, He will (1 Peter 1:5). When He promises to work life's circumstances together for your good, He will (Romans 8:28). What an amazing assurance is ours because of our faithful and powerful God!

Another observation in today's reading is that Jesus had a scriptural reply each time the devil tempted Him in the wilderness. This teaches us of the importance of Scripture memory.

Thank You, Lord, for always making good on Your promises. You are trustworthy and sovereign, and I praise You for that. I'm humbled by the fact that You devised a plan long before You created me to rescue my soul for eternity—thank You.

"Then saith Jesus unto him, Get thee hence, Satan: for it is written, Thou shalt worship the Lord thy God, and him only shalt thou serve."

Matthew 4:10

DAY 2

MATTHEW 5–7

Jesus' First Recorded Sermon

OVERVIEW

When we finished chapter 4, Jesus had just emerged on the scene of public life at 30 years old, speaking in Jewish synagogues, calling His disciples, and beginning to heal people. Now, in chapters 5–7, He delivers the Sermon on the Mount, turning much of the man-made Jewish religious practice on its head. In contrast to the Pharisees, who were fixed on external religiosity, Jesus called His followers to a different faith life—a dynamic pursuit of the Father, from the heart. This stands out in a series of contrasting statements, "Ye have heard…but I say…" (5:21 27, 31, 33, 38, 43). This sermon set Jesus apart from any Jewish teacher this audience had ever heard.

DEVOTIONAL APPLICATION

Though given 2,000 years ago, this sermon remains highly applicable to us today. The humility conveyed in the beatitudes (5:3–12), our responsibility to shine as lights (5:16), the issue of materialism (6:24–33), and the warning against hypocrisy (7:1–5) are all themes that speak to our lives. As you read, let Jesus' words sink in where most needed.

The sections of this sermon that always seem to challenge me the most are those on prayer. D. L. Moody said, "Next to the wonder of seeing my Saviour will be, I think, the wonder that I made so little use of the power of prayer."

Think of the promise in 6:6, "When thou prayest, enter into thy closet…and thy Father which seeth in secret shall reward thee openly." Then in 7:11, "If ye then, being evil, know how to give good gifts unto your children, how much more shall your Father which is in heaven give good things to them that ask him?"

Prayer is one of those areas where most of us have room to grow. What step can you take today to make greater use of prayer? Jesus didn't say, "*If* you pray." He said, "*When* you pray" (6:5,6,7).

Lord Jesus, You encouraged us to "ask, seek, and knock." And You've promised that we will receive, find, and see the door opened. Please help me to experience the glorious miracle of answered prayer. I know I've been guilty of asking too little and too seldom in the past. Please draw me to You, and I ask with the disciples, "Teach me to pray."

"Ask, and it shall be given you; seek, and ye shall find; knock, and it shall be opened unto you: For every one that asketh receiveth; and he that seeketh findeth; and to him that knocketh it shall be opened."

Matthew 7:7–8

DAY 3

MATTHEW 8–10

Jesus Demonstrates His Power over Physical and Spiritual Realms

OVERVIEW

The earthly ministry of Jesus moved through seasons orchestrated with precision and purpose, according to the sovereign plan of God. Today's Scripture section records a time of swelling popularity (it would not always be this way) as people were drawn to Christ's miracles and messages. Nine times Jesus exercised His power and authority: over physical illness (8:1–17), over the weather (8:23–27), and over demons (8:28–33). Finally, Jesus exercised the greatest power of all—a clear demonstration of His deity—when He forgave sins (9:1–8).

APPLICATION

Consider what the recipients of Jesus' miracles must have felt, when their tragedies were turned into God-glorifying triumphs. I imagine that the joy and relief they experienced were immeasurable. There are many miracle recipients we do not know of, but the ones recorded in this portion of Scripture seem to reveal a pattern for us. The pattern is *faith:* "I have not found so great faith, no not in Israel" (8:10); "Jesus seeing their faith" (9:2); "thy faith hath made thee whole" (9:22); "According to your faith be it unto you" (9:29).

Don't misunderstand. It was Jesus' power—not their faith—that accomplished the miracles. I reject the televangelist's message that if we just have enough faith, we can demand health and wealth from God. That's a shallow, one-dimensional, and unbiblical concept of faith.

But let's not forget, God does respond to the faith of His people. He delights in faith. He has recorded in His Word many extraordinary things that were accomplished "by faith." (Check out Hebrews 11.) Are you trusting in God for the needs in your life?

Perhaps God wants us to take a cue from the recipients of miracles in Matthew's Gospel. Is God inviting you to take a step that depends on His miracle-working power? Is there a prayer He wants you to pray, an individual He wants you to witness to, a matter of stewardship that requires your trust in Him? Let's approach today with the spirit of the eighteenth-century missionary, William Carey, who said, "Expect great things from God; attempt great things for God."

Jesus is worthy of your faith. And He will respond to your faith. You may not always understand His ways, and He may not always answer your requests the way you expect, but He is powerful and faithful and good—and you can trust Him.

Lord Jesus, I praise You for Your power and authority exercised over every realm in the universe. You're amazing! And I thank You that this same power is exercised in my life today, even though I don't always see or sense it. I trust You, that You're working, that You're in charge, and that You're powerful. Help me today to attempt great things for You and expect great things from You. I believe You are able.

"Then touched he their eyes, saying, According to your faith be it unto you."

Matthew 9:29

DAY 4

MATTHEW 11–13

As Forces of Opposition Emerge, Jesus Reveals the Uniqueness of His Kingdom

OVERVIEW

Today's passage doesn't digest as quickly and naturally as the first ten chapters of Matthew due to its discussion of first-century Jewish culture and its numerous parables. But that's okay. Hang in there! This is one of those passages to read slowly, knowing that each time you come back to it, you'll understand more. Be on the lookout for principles and applications that you *do* understand. In today's passage, we see the religious ruling class of Jesus' day, the Scribes and Pharisees, begin to question Jesus and plot against Him. Because they saw Him as a threat to their power, they sought to discredit Him. But Jesus was not intimidated, and He was always one giant step ahead of them whenever they engaged Him.

APPLICATION

There are two great applications in this passage. The first concerns *our words,* and the second concerns *God's Word.*

We find an insightful principle in 12:34, when Jesus says, "out of the abundance of the heart the mouth speaketh." The source of our words is our hearts. The Bible has much to say about the importance of our words. How do you speak to others—in your home, at your workplace, in the public square, and in your church? Words matter. Jesus says in verse 36 that we will give an account one day for every idle (careless) word we've ever spoken. That's sobering. According to Jesus, if I want my words to be good, I need to cultivate a good heart. That's one benefit of saturating our minds and hearts in the Bible daily.

This brings us to the second application in this passage—*God's Word.* In the parable of the sower (13:18–23), Jesus explained that God's Word, planted in the soil of our hearts, causes our lives to become fruitful. Jesus spoke of four types of soil as representing four types of hearts. Only one kind of heart allows the Word of God to flourish—a receptive, sincere, and hungry heart that allows Scripture to put down deep roots.

That's what this ninety-day journey is all about! It's about letting God's Word sink deeply into our hearts so that we might bear fruit for His glory.

Thank You, Lord, for the good seed of Your Word. As I receive it today into my heart and mind, I ask You to produce fruit upward as You deepen Your roots downward. I trust You will improve the condition of my heart so that my words—and all that proceeds from me—become *good* because of Your influence in my life.

"A good man out of the good treasure of the heart bringeth forth good things: and an evil man out of the evil treasure bringeth forth evil things."

Matthew 12:35

DAY 5

MATTHEW 14–16

Jesus with the Disciples, the Multitudes, and the Religious Leaders

OVERVIEW

The opposition to Jesus continues in today's passage, but that's not all. The miracles continue as well as Jesus feeds thousands, walks on water, and heals countless afflicted people. Jesus' preparation of His disciples continues too. Jesus begins to prepare them for what lies ahead—the cross where He would sacrifice His life for the sins of mankind.

DEVOTIONAL APPLICATION

The miracles and parables of Jesus led the disciples to the realization that He was indeed the prophesied Messiah. Peter said it well: "Thou art the Christ, the Son of the living God" in 16:16. But the disciples were swept up in the same common misconception that many Jews held concerning the Messiah—that he would be a political or military saviour. But Jesus knew what kind of Saviour He came to be—a suffering, sacrificing, atoning Saviour—a Saviour on a cross. He "began to show" this to His disciples (16:21).

One of the most difficult things for the disciples to accept was that following a Saviour with a cross meant that they, too, would have crosses of their own. Jesus said, "If any man will come after me, let him deny himself, and take up his cross, and follow me" (16:24). This is counter-intuitive. Who knowingly signs up for something that involves pain? Jesus did. And He calls us to do the same. To follow Jesus is a great joy, but He made it clear that it would also involve suffering.

What suffering might He be calling on you to endure for His glory and kingdom today? Have you been labeled a religious fanatic at work for simply being a witness?

Are you struggling with an unwanted illness that is within the sovereign plan of God? Is there a difficult and stressful situation in a relationship or in your finances?

Whatever it is, just remember when you're in the middle of it that Jesus' story didn't end on the cross. It ended in triumph, and so will yours. Check out 16:21 again where Jesus predicted His cross. The last seven words are "and be raised again the third day." Take up your cross—whatever it is. Jesus will accomplish His purposes through it and see you through to victory, just as He did with His cross.

Jesus, it's my privilege to follow You. Sometimes I think following You should be easy and painless, but that's shortsighted of me. Help me be willing to suffer for You. I thank You for the extraordinary suffering that You endured on my behalf. Please grant me the grace, strength, and patience that I need when following You requires me to endure suffering.

"Then said Jesus unto his disciples, If any man will come after me, let him deny himself, and take up his cross, and follow me."

Matthew 16:24

DAY 6

MATTHEW 17–19

Jesus Reveals His Divine Glory and Values

OVERVIEW

Chapter 17 opens with the record of Jesus providing a glimpse of His heavenly glory to His inner circle of disciples. Following this transfiguration, Jesus begins to help his disciples understand His values concerning prayer and fasting (17:14–21), greatness and children (18:1–14), personal conflict (18:15–20), forgiveness (18:23–35), marriage (19:1–12), and possessions (19:16–30). The disciples discover that Jesus sees things far differently than unsaved people in the surrounding culture.

APPLICATION

How much of yourself do you see in the lives of the disciples throughout these scenes? They had so much to learn. So do we.

For instance, Peter might have expected to impress the Lord when he asked whether it was sufficient to forgive his brother seven times (18:21). Instead, Jesus said he was only seven thousand percent off. Then Jesus gave one of his most lengthy and relatable parables—the parable of the unforgiving servant (18:23–35).

The message of this parable is crystal clear for those who have received Christ. God has relieved us of an enormous debt, which would have been impossible to repay in a thousand lifetimes (the parable's amount is roughly $10 billion in today's economy) and which would have brought down unthinkable wrath upon us. But only through a merciful act from our Lord, we have been completely forgiven of it all.

But what about when someone wrongs us? However sizable the offense, Jesus implies it can never amount to what He has already forgiven us (about $200 compared to $10 billion). It would be ridiculous, wouldn't it, if someone who had just been forgiven a $10 billion debt would turn around and harass someone who owed him

$200? But that's how it is, according to Jesus, when Christians refuse to forgive those who wrong them.

C. S. Lewis said, "To be a Christian means to forgive the inexcusable because God has forgiven the inexcusable in you." Forgiveness is essentially my decision to release my wrongdoer from retribution. The best practical definition I've come across is from biblical counselor Jay Adams: "Forgiveness is making a promise to not bring up the offense again—to the one who wronged you, to others, or to yourself."

Is there someone in your life you have refused to forgive? If so, you know what you need to do. Jesus didn't say it would be easy. But forgiving you wasn't easy for Him either.

Jesus, I could never thank You enough for forgiving the great sin debt I owed You. Thank You for Your compassionate heart and pity toward me. I understand that You expect me to extend that same forgiveness toward those who wrong me. Please grant me Your enabling grace to obey this command.

"Shouldest not thou also have had compassion on thy fellowservant, even as I had pity on thee?"

Matthew 18:33

DAY 7

MATTHEW 20–22

Upon Jesus' Triumphant Entry into Jerusalem, Tensions Escalate

OVERVIEW

Jesus predicts, for the third time, His own death and resurrection (20:17–19; the first two are 16:21 and 17:22–23)—a clear indication of His deity. He re-enters Jerusalem to the jubilant cheering of the Jewish people (21:1–11), signaling the fulfillment of prophecy and the final week before His crucifixion. He cleanses the Temple of its profiteers, which leads to a series of confrontations by the sub-sects of the religious ruling class. Jesus responds to their interrogations with parables and questions of His own, an action which not only confound their attempts to discredit Him, but also intensify their desire to destroy Him.

APPLICATION

Jesus predicts His crucifixion again, but this time in more heart-wrenching detail. You might expect the disciples to respond with empathy or concern. Yet they only had themselves in mind. Brothers James and John convinced their mother to ask Jesus for cabinet positions in what they (incorrectly) saw as His soon-to-come earthly Kingdom. The other disciples were thinking along the same lines, though these brothers beat them to the request.

Jesus proceeded to help them understand the true path to His definition of greatness. The culture of those who do not know God ("the Gentiles" in 20:25) defines greatness as having authority over others—it's a *position to achieve.* In Christ's kingdom, however, greatness is a *posture to assume*—that of a servant: "...whosoever will be great among you, let him be your minister; And whosoever will be chief among you, let him be your servant" (20:26–27).

According to Jesus, if you want to be great, start finding ways to serve. Someone said, "Greatness is measured not by how many people serve you, but rather by how many people you serve."

Jesus was the ultimate example of this greatness that is servanthood. The very next verses record Him stopping His journey at the request of two blind outcasts and, to paraphrase 20:32, asking them, "How can I serve you?" A few days later, He would wash the disciples' feet. And the next day, He would serve all mankind by carrying our sins to the cross (Philippians 2:5–8). What a servant our Saviour was!

Over the past twenty years, I've seen pastors, deacons, musicians, church volunteers, and Christian professors try to seek greatness the Gentiles' way by achieving a position. Does it surprise you that it never turned out well? But thankfully, I've seen far more Christians seek Jesus' way by pursuing ways to serve others.

Choose to be great; choose to be a servant.

Jesus, thank You for Your wonderful example of what servanthood looks like. Even Your very act of coming to earth in the incarnation was an extraordinary act of service. Forgive me for my tendency to only serve those who I think might return good to me. And thank You most of all for serving me by dying on the cross on my behalf. May I serve others by sharing with them that great news of salvation.

"Even as the Son of man came not to be ministered unto, but to minister, and to give his life a ransom for many."

Matthew 20:28

DAY 8

MATTHEW 23–25

Rebuking the Pharisees, Prophesying the Future, Defining the Kingdom

OVERVIEW

Until this point, the Pharisees had been the antagonists. But in chapter 23, Jesus calls them out in a public condemnation of their hypocrisy. Then, chapters 24–25 contain "The Olivet Discourse." Here Jesus shares with His disciples signs concerning the destruction of Jerusalem and His ultimate future return (two separate, future events), followed by five "kingdom parables" to help the disciples understand the importance of being faithful, watchful servants upon His departure.

APPLICATION

As Jesus mentored the disciples—the future leaders of His church—it was important to Him that they not use the Scribes and Pharisees as their pattern for spiritual leadership. Jesus' words were, "Do not ye after their works" (23:3). Jesus then publicly outlined seven characteristics of a Pharisee. I've added three characteristics from chapter 15 to bring the list to an even ten:

- They don't practice what they preach (23:3).
- They burden people down instead of help people up (23:4).
- They perform their duties only to impress others (23:5–7).
- They make it difficult for people to come to God (23:13).
- They major on God's minors and minor on God's majors (23:24).
- They manufacture external, man-made signs of holiness (23:5b, 25–28).
- They disregard their own internal sinfulness (23:25–28).
- They value tradition over God's commands (15:6).

- They allow religious words to replace sincere hearts (15:8).
- They presumptuously teach men's commands as doctrine (15:9).

Instead, Jesus is looking for leaders who will patiently, faithfully serve their Lord like those exemplified in the kingdom parables. These are leaders who will

- Dutifully watch for their master's return, remembering that they're accountable to him (24:44–45).
- Humbly, diligently tend to their responsibilities, knowing that they're doing it for him (25:21).
- Help the hungry, thirsty, strangers, naked, sick and imprisoned, as an act of service unto him (25:35–36).

Jesus isn't looking for fancy Pharisees. He's looking for faithful servants.

Lord Jesus, thank You for calling me to be Your servant. I feel like I'm in the audience with Your first disciples as You instruct Your servants. Forgive me for being undependable at times. Help me now, going forward, to be a faithful, watchful servant, who carries out Your work with the spiritual diligence it deserves. I do look forward to Your return, and to the joy of entering Your presence to celebrate with You for all of eternity.

"His lord said unto him, Well done, thou good and faithful servant: thou hast been faithful over a few things, I will make thee ruler over many things: enter thou into the joy of thy lord."

Matthew 25:21

DAY 9

MATTHEW 26–28

Jesus Betrayed, Tried, Denied, Crucified, and Risen

OVERVIEW

Chapter 26 records the final two days before Jesus' sacrifice on the cross. Judas betrays Jesus by arranging for His arrest. Jesus shares a Passover meal with His disciples in the upper room and then agonizes in prayer in the Garden of Gethsemane until His arrest by a Jewish mob. Jesus is taken to the priestly palace where He is interrogated. In chapter 27, His custody is handed over from the Jewish religious leaders to the Roman regional governor, Pilate. At the demand of the Jewish leaders and mob, Pilate directs Jesus to be beaten, crucified, and buried. Finally, in chapter 28, Jesus rises from the grave, once and for all demonstrating His deity, and gives marching orders to His amazed and grateful disciples.

APPLICATION

Approaching chapters 26–28 is like walking on holy ground. It contains the most heart-wrenching, agonizing story in the Bible. But it's the most important story of the Bible—the climax of all the stories. God, as man, willingly offers Himself as a substitute, on a wicked and shameful cross, for the sins of all mankind. The plan of God for man's redemption arrived at its destination—Calvary.

Whenever I read about Christ's humiliation and suffering, I'm reminded of a sobering truth—that my sin put Jesus in that place. The shame and pain He experienced on that day is directly because of me—my selfish, rebellious deeds. This ought to make me profoundly grateful to Him for what He endured that day, driven by love for me. It ought to humble me.

It also ought to make me so disgusted by sin that I reject it. When I'm tempted to sin, I should remember that day. I don't want to have any more part in what put my Saviour through that agony. Jesus—who endured the whipping, shaming, and agony—now walks beside me as my Friend, having cleansed, forgiven, and granted me a lifetime and eternity filled with the joys His death secured for me.

If He was willing to do that for us, we ought to be willing to tell people about Him. The last words recorded by Matthew are the instructions Jesus gave to the disciples, who like us, had just been the recipients of the greatest gift. Those instructions were to "Go," and spread the message of salvation.

Lord Jesus, thank You for willingly taking my punishment and bearing the cross for my sin. Because of Your suffering, I don't have to face eternal punishment. I praise You for coming out of that grave, victorious over death. Thank You for being my Saviour, who not only died for me, but shares new life with me.

"Go ye therefore, and teach all nations, baptizing them in the name of the Father, and of the Son, and of the Holy Ghost: Teaching them to observe all things whatsoever I have commanded you: and, lo, I am with you alway, even unto the end of the world. Amen."

Matthew 28:19–20

DAY 10

MARK 1–3

Jesus Heals Those in Need, Teaches Eager Listeners, and Commissions His Disciples

OVERVIEW

Mark is the fast–paced Gospel. The shortest of the four records, it's jam-packed with scenes from the life of our Lord, moving quickly from one to the next. By the time we get to verse 13, Jesus is 30 years old and has already been baptized and overcome the devil's temptation (events you'll recall from Matthew chapters 3 and 4). Jesus begins calling His disciples, healing countless who suffer with disease or demons, and teaching in the synagogue. The conflict with the religious leaders surfaces quickly, over Jesus' actions on the Sabbath.

APPLICATION

Mark records a long, busy, and productive Sabbath day in our Lord's ministry, in 1:21–34. It begins with teaching in the synagogue, where Jesus delivers a man from being possessed of demons. Then, after healing Peter's mother-in-law, He heals many others and delivers more from demonic possession, working into the night (v. 32). He healed so many, in fact, that they lost count—the whole city, it seems, was there (v. 33).

The next day's itinerary was similar. Everyone was looking for Jesus (v. 37). There would be more traveling on foot, more preaching, more healing, more delivering from demons. But an important thing happened, before sunrise, on that following day. Jesus "went out, and departed into a solitary place, and there prayed" (1:35). The Son of God, the Creator of the universe, chose to spend the early part of the day in prayer—in fellowship with his Father. What an example for us!

The demands of life are nonstop for the believer. As students, parents, teachers, pastors, church leaders, employees, neighbors, grandparents, friends and citizens—

there will always be one more person to help and one more project to complete. Just like in the life of Jesus, one full day of exhausting ministry will often be followed by another.

Jesus took on a human body, and though He was fully divine, He was subject to the same physical and emotional wear and tear as we are. Later, Paul encouraged the believers, that in light of this *outward* toil, our *inward* man must be renewed each day (2 Corinthians 4:16).

Instead of foolishly racing into the demands of the day without prayer, let's stop and carve out solitary time in fellowship with our Father. If we start our day by taking the issues of the day to the Lord, we are already infinitely farther ahead than if we had started tackling them in our own power, because we invite the involvement of our all-powerful, all-wise God, who promises to hear and answer our prayers.

Lord Jesus, I recognize that the call to be Your disciple is first a call to be with You and then a call to serve You. Forgive me for so often rushing into my duties without prayer...as if I don't need You. As You spent time with the Father during Your earthly ministry, may I also fellowship with You and the Father each day. I trust You to make Your presence real to me, drawing near to me as I draw near to You.

"And in the morning, rising up a great while before day, he went out, and departed into a solitary place, and there prayed."

Mark 1:35

DAY 11

MARK 4–6

Jesus Tells Parables and Performs Miracles around Galilee's Coast

OVERVIEW

The fast pace continues in Mark 4–6. After telling several important parables, Jesus and the disciples cross the Sea of Galilee to the region of Gadara, where He delivers a tormented, cemetery-dwelling soul. They return to heal a diseased woman and to raise Jairus' daughter. Jesus sends His disciples on a preaching and healing crusade, the miraculous results of which capture the attention of Herod, who assumes John the Baptist had resurrected from a death that he ordered. Jesus feeds the five thousand and for a second time calms a storm while on board a ship on the Sea of Galilee.

APPLICATION

Boats are a common feature in today's passage: Jesus teaches from a boat. He sleeps in a boat during a storm. He crisscrosses Galilee numerous times in a boat. He walks on water while the disciples are tossed about in a boat.

We learn an important principle as we observe the Lord's interaction with His disciples while boating (chapters 4 and 6): you can't be full of *fear* and full of *faith* at the same time (4:40). When the disciples alerted Jesus to the storm, He had already told them they were headed to the other side (4:35). When Jesus states His plans, you can count on them. And when He's on board, you can rest confidently.

In both storms, the disciples needed a greater level of confidence in Jesus—greater faith in what He could do in their lives. That's our need too. We don't need more of Jesus. (If we've received Him as Saviour, we've received Him fully!) We simply need more confidence in Jesus—we need greater faith.

The truth is Jesus has already provided us with all the evidence we need to place our faith in Him. Can you think back to prayers He has answered, problems He has solved, provision He has given, and breakthroughs He has provided? The disciples' surprise that Jesus was able to calm the first storm (4:41) was understandable. But why were they shocked the second time He calmed a storm (6:51)? Mark records the reason: "their heart was hardened" (6:52).

If these disciples' hearts were hardened, after all that they had seen and experienced while traveling with Jesus, your heart and mine could become hardened too. The solution? Remind yourself what God has done. Count your blessings. Read the Word (Romans 10:17). It will soften your heart and increase your faith. And as we learned in Matthew 8–9 (on Day 3), faith will allow you to receive the good things God wants to accomplish through you.

Lord Jesus, forgive me for my lack of faith in You. You've done so much to deserve my confidence and trust. And yet I'm still often fearful. Thank You for the miracles You've accomplished in my life, the greatest of which is my salvation. May I be mindful of Your sovereignty and omnipotence at work in every situation for my good.

"And he said unto them, Why are ye so fearful? how is it that ye have no faith?"

Mark 4:40

DAY 12

MARK 7–9

Christ's Divine Power Becomes More Fully Displayed to the Disciples

OVERVIEW

The first half of chapter 7 exposes the hypocrisy of the Pharisees as Jesus corrects their religious misconceptions. Then, Jesus casts out a demon, heals a deaf mute, feeds four thousand, and gives sight to the blind. On two occasions, Jesus predicts His death and resurrection to the disciples and calls on them to take up their own crosses and follow Him. After His transfiguration, Jesus delivers a demon-possessed boy whom the disciples were unable to help.

APPLICATION

Three sad words summarize the spiritual impotence of the disciples: "they could not" (9:18). They had previously been sent two by two with some success, healing and teaching and casting out demons (6:7). But on this day, "they could not." They were powerless to help the father who had brought his desperately tormented son to them.

Those words could be used to describe us on many occasions. We're trying to make a difference, overcome a sin, repair a relationship, see someone saved, or solve a problem. And it could be said of us, "they could not." Have you been confronted with your own incapability?

What was their problem? What's ours? Jesus answered it with one revealing word: *faithless* (9:19). Jesus explained to the disciples and the boy's father that the key to the son's deliverance would be faith. "If thou canst believe, all things are possible to him that believeth" (9:23).

Then, Jesus revealed to the disciples how this faith is practiced—by prayer and fasting. When the disciples asked, "Why could not we cast him out?" Jesus said, "This kind can come forth by nothing, but by prayer and fasting" (9:29). Apparently, there is a direct link between believing prayer and spiritual power.

Prayer and fasting are to spiritual power what weightlifting is to physical power. And faith is the muscle. The more we exercise the muscle of faith by prayer and fasting, the stronger and more powerful its potential becomes. Want strong faith? Give yourself to prayer.

E. Stanley Jones, a missionary to India in the early twentieth century, said it this way: "When prayer fades out, power fades out. We are as spiritual as we are prayerful; no more, no less."

Is there an unusually large need in some area of your life? According to Jesus, the simple answer is found in prayer and fasting.

Lord Jesus, it's reassuring that though the boy's deliverance was beyond Your disciples' power, it was not beyond Yours. I realize that it's Your will to share and display that power in my life. I want to be empowered by You. Give me the strength to pray and also to fast when necessary. More than anything, I want to experience the fullness of Your power in my life.

"And he said unto them, This kind can come forth by nothing, but by prayer and fasting."

Mark 9:29

DAY 13

MARK 10–12

Jesus' Path Is Directed toward Jerusalem and Beyond

OVERVIEW

Chapter 10 contains Jesus' teaching on the sanctity of marriage, the value of children, the dilemma of riches, and the definition of greatness. In all of these areas, common culture had it wrong, just as it does today. Jesus then enters Jerusalem for His final confrontations with the religious rulers, which ultimately lead to His betrayal and death.

APPLICATION

In chapter 12, each religious group—the Pharisees, Herodians, Sadducees, and scribes—lines up to take its turn to stump Jesus with religious riddles. One of the more complex questions came from a scribe who said, "Which is the first [most important] commandment of all?" (12:28). There were, during that time, 613 commands carefully followed by faithful Jews. How could you possibly catalog and prioritize them on the spot?

But Jesus' answer was immediate: "Thou shalt love the Lord thy God with all thy heart, and with all thy soul, and with all thy mind, and with all thy strength." And once again, Jesus won the debate. His answer was simple but profound. It was also an indictment because this loving affection for the Lord had been lost among the outward-oriented Jewish religious adherents. Their hearts, Jesus said, were far from God.

As believers in the church age, we don't have a rigid set of commands to which we must adhere. We do, however, have many principles and instructions in the New Testament which we are obligated to obey.

Let Jesus' answer remind you where to start in your journey of obedience. All the other commands "hang on" this command to love God. If you keep all the rules but don't love God, you've missed everything. If, however, you pursue a deepening love for the Lord, you'll likely find the guidance and motivation to do the other things the Lord expects of you.

Our responsibility to witness, our call to holiness, to biblical obedience in our words, actions, attitudes, priorities, and all areas of the Christian life begin with love for Christ. So let's deepen our love for Him through meditation on His words and fellowship with Him in prayer.

Father, deepen my love for You each day. I want to show my love to You through loyal obedience and faithful service. Thank You for loving me first. As I seek to draw nearer to You, I trust You'll also draw nearer to me in love. Thank You for promising to do just that.

"And thou shalt love the Lord thy God with all thy heart, and with all thy soul, and with all thy mind, and with all thy strength: this is the first commandment."

Mark 12:30

DAY 14

MARK 13–16

Mark's Fast-Paced Account Slows to Capture the Detail of Christ's Sacrifice

OVERVIEW

While the earlier part of Mark's Gospel moves quickly from event to event, the closing chapters slow down to describe a detailed account of the betrayal, trial, and crucifixion of our Lord. In chapter 13, Jesus prepares His disciples for a future without His physical presence. Chapter 14 records Jesus' time with His disciples in the upper room, Judas' betrayal, Gethsemane and Christ's arrest. Chapter 15 details the crucifixion, and chapter 16 resumes the fast-paced narrative describing the Lord's resurrection and His meeting with the disciples.

Historians believe that the apostle Peter was the primary eyewitness for the contents of Mark's Gospel record. Think of Peter's perspective as you read today's narrative, and it will add clarity as you envision the events that unfold.

APPLICATION

Jesus took great care to prepare His disciples for His ultimate ascension back to Heaven, which would occur just forty days after His resurrection. Chapter 13 includes one of these conversations between Christ and the disciples. Between the time of His departure and His ultimate future return, Jesus knew that human nature would tempt His followers to become careless toward their spiritual responsibilities so He gave them an analogy: "For the Son of man is as a man taking a far journey, who left his house, and gave authority to his servants, and to every man his work….Watch ye therefore: for ye know not when the master of the house cometh…Lest coming suddenly he find you sleeping" (13:34–36).

Jesus wants every generation of His followers—not just the first disciples—to live in a manner that eagerly anticipates His return. This includes active service, faithful prayer, and spiritual alertness. This passage reveals that Jesus has given each of His servants specific responsibilities. And it is Christ's desire that, upon His return, He would not find His servants "sleeping on the job."

What area of your Christian life is lacking? Witnessing to someone who needs the Lord? Faithful giving as a steward of your finances? Your prayer life? Finding a ministry in your church? I'm sure if you take a moment to ask the Lord, He'll reveal—by His Spirit and perhaps through today's reading—exactly what you need to do in order to be ready if He returns today.

We don't know exactly when He'll return. Let's be ready!

Lord Jesus, I look forward to Your return. Help me to be ready for it. Show me the areas in my life that are lacking, and enable me to address them that I may be found faithful and fruitful until Your coming.

"For the Son of man is as a man taking a far journey, who left his house, and gave authority to his servants, and to every man his work, and commanded the porter to watch."

Mark 13:34

DAY 15

LUKE 1–3

The Miraculous Birth of the Prophesied Messiah and His Prophesied Forerunner

OVERVIEW

While Mark's Gospel is the shortest and fastest-paced, Luke's Gospel is the opposite—the longest and most detailed. Each Gospel writer was guided by the Holy Spirit for each word and their overlapping yet unique accounts complete our portrait of Christ, each contributing a different combination of events. Luke was a medical doctor and loyal traveling companion of the apostle Paul. He took great care to assemble a chronological (1:1, 3) and detailed biography of our Lord's earthly life, based on the eyewitness accounts of the apostles (1:2).

Luke starts with the details surrounding John the Baptist's miraculous birth—his parents suffered from infertility and were senior citizens. He ties this miracle in with the events taking place at the same time, with John's mother Elisabeth and her cousin, Mary, and the details of an even greater miracle taking place within her—Christ's virgin birth.

Luke 3:23–38 contain Jesus' genealogy on Mary's side (Joseph, the husband's name, was used in her stead, a common Jewish practice at that time).

APPLICATION

It's easy to admire John the Baptist for his combination of rugged boldness and humble faithfulness, and for so diligently pointing people to the Saviour. Consider his words to his audience at the Jordan River: "Bring forth therefore fruits worthy of repentance" (3:8). In other words, John said, "Actions speak louder than words."

It's one thing to say you're a believer, but it's another thing to demonstrate that reality on a daily basis. Israel had departed from God with unbelieving, unfaithful hearts. John's ministry was to call them to repentance in preparation for the coming Messiah. But John said, "Let's see some evidence—some fruit—of repentance in your life." In 3:10 his audience asked, "What shall we do then?" The answer was four-fold:

- John called the Pharisees to *humility*. "Begin not to say within yourselves, We have Abraham to our father" (3:8).
- He called the common people to *generosity*. "He that hath two coats, let him impart to him that hath none;" (3:11).
- He called the publicans (tax collectors) to *integrity*. "Exact no more than that which is appointed you" (3:13).
- And He called the soldiers to *sincerity*. "Do violence to no man, neither accuse falsely; and be content with your wages" (3:14).

Humility, generosity, integrity, sincerity—John just as easily could have been speaking to a twenty-first-century audience. These character traits don't come naturally to us. Rather, they're marks of regeneration by the Spirit of God—fruits of repentance. And God calls us to pursue them daily.

Father, it's my desire to demonstrate a life of sincere repentance and faith toward You. Search me today and identify areas that are out of line with the fruit that You would expect in me. Before You, I want to *be right* and then *live rightly* as an outward expression. Thank You for Your enabling grace as I pursue this reality.

"Bring forth therefore fruits worthy of repentance...."

Luke 3:8

DAY 16

LUKE 4–6

Jesus Demonstrates His Power over Temptation, Disease, Demons, and the Religious Establishment

OVERVIEW

Chapter 4 opens with Jesus' temptation by Satan in the wilderness. From there, He captures the attention of the Galilean residents—first through His teaching in the synagogues and then through the countless people He heals or delivers from demon possession. The Jewish leaders begin to confront Jesus and His disciples over their pet issues, such as hand-washing, fasting, and the Sabbath. Unintimidated by their disapproval, Jesus gives the Sermon on the Mount.

APPLICATION

Do any of these statements sound familiar?

"You scratch my back, I'll scratch yours."

"God helps those who help themselves."

"I don't get mad, I get even."

"You owe me one."

These are not statements rooted in Christian thinking. Instead, they are rooted in the selfish, sinful nature of humankind. And one of the great purposes of Jesus' Sermon on the Mount was to help His listeners realize that His way of thinking was different from mankind's flawed ways.

Jesus said, "Love your enemies, do good to them which hate you, bless them that curse you, and pray for them which despitefully use you" (6:27–28). "Give to every man that asketh of thee" (6:30). And be "kind unto the unthankful and to the evil" (6:35). None of these behaviors come naturally to us.

To paraphrase Jesus in 6:32–34, it's easy to love people who love you, do good to those who do good to you, and lend to those who will repay you. But where's the merit in any of that? Where's the grace in that? That's not being Christlike; that's just being *human*. And Jesus calls us to a higher standard of treatment of others than the human standard. He calls us to abandon our self-interest and do what He did—throw ourselves into blessing others with no expectation of return.

How do we find the motivation to do this? I can think of only two reasons: First, Jesus commanded us. Second, He showed us what it looked like through His life and by taking the punishment for our sin on the cross. The recipients of our grace may not be worthy of it, but Christ is.

Lord Jesus, only You are worthy to instruct me in my treatment of others. You led by example, and I want to obey Your commandments. Help me identify situations in which I have the opportunity to obey these instructions. Give me the grace to treat others as You have treated me.

"But love ye your enemies, and do good, and lend, hoping for nothing again; and your reward shall be great, and ye shall be the children of the Highest: for he is kind unto the unthankful and to the evil."

Luke 6:35

DAY 17

LUKE 7–9

Jesus Transforms Lives, Trains His Disciples, and Is Transfigured

OVERVIEW

These chapters record an extraordinary amount of ministry performed by our miracle-working Lord. Many are healed, including a centurion's servant and a diseased woman. Jesus calms a storm at sea, casts out demons, and raises Jairus' daughter from the dead. He feeds the five thousand and raises a deceased son. Jesus also shares numerous lessons with His disciples to prepare them for His coming death and Kingdom.

APPLICATION

One of the most memorable miracles in our Lord's ministry was the deliverance of the maniac of Gadara. Parallel passages (Matthew 8:28–34, Mark 5:1–20) indicate there were actually two men who received deliverance, but Mark and Luke share only the one. Chains couldn't hold this wild man. He was possessed by hundreds—maybe thousands—of demons. This amazing story yields three lessons for us to remember:

First, those who have been rescued by Jesus are radically transformed. Verse 35 of chapter 8 records, "They went out to see…and found the man…sitting at the feet of Jesus, clothed, and in his right mind…." Are the observable character traits of your life different as a result of coming face to face with Jesus Christ? They should be.

Second, observers aren't always eager to accept the radical transformation that Christ brings. Verse 35 says "they were afraid" and verse 37 says they "besought [Jesus] to depart from them; for they were taken with great fear." The reality is that people who don't know God don't always celebrate the change Jesus brings. Spiritual matters are lost on them.

Third, people whose lives have been transformed by Jesus have a story to share. "And he went his way, and published throughout the whole city how great things

Jesus had done unto him" (8:39). The fact that some people didn't understand didn't keep the changed man silent—he was thrilled that his life had been miraculously rescued by the Son of God! He didn't need the public's approval to share his story. Neither do you.

His testimony resonated with some. Yours will, too. When Jesus re-visited this region later in His ministry, a great multitude gathered to hear Him teach (see Mark 7:31–8:9). I suspect that these people's eagerness to know Jesus Christ was due, in part, to the vibrant testimony of this transformed man!

Jesus, thank You for rescuing me from a life of hopelessness. I may not have been demon possessed, but I was certainly headed to Hell and bound for an eternity without You. I was as lost as the maniac of Gadara until You came into my life, saved my soul, and transformed me. Please grant me boldness and ignite my passion to share the greatness of Your saving grace with those around me. Use me as Your witness even today.

"Return to thine own house, and shew how great things God hath done unto thee. And he went his way, and published throughout the whole city how great things Jesus had done unto him."

Luke 8:39

DAY 18

LUKE 10–12

Jesus Deputizes Evangelists, Teaches the Masses, and Confronts the Pharisees

OVERVIEW

Jesus had already sent the twelve disciples in pairs to preach and heal. Now He sends seventy in the same manner. Then, in response to a man's insistence on his own righteousness, Jesus relates the classic story of the good Samaritan. He teaches His disciples about the essence and importance of prayer. Finally, Jesus confronts the Pharisees for their hypocrisy and helps a large crowd understand the great value of the eternal and heavenly over the temporal and earthly.

APPLICATION

Mankind's perspective on earthly possessions and pleasure was completely flawed in Jesus' day and has grown even more extreme today. Most people—including Christians—tend to define *success* in terms of material possessions, interesting experiences, or self-indulgent pleasures. The ultimate, if you could attain it, would be to have it all, do it all, and experience it all.

What this perspective misses is not only that material things don't satisfy but also that, even if they did, they could not possibly extend that satisfaction into eternity. As the simple saying goes, "you can't take it with you." We claim to understand that, but our behaviors and priorities indicate we don't.

Jesus' parables and principles in chapter 12 remind us of the following:

- The eternal is of greater consequence than the temporal.
- The spiritual is of greater importance than the physical.
- The heavenly is of greater value than the earthly.

God does indeed give us physical provision and enjoyable opportunities as generous gifts from His benevolent hand (12:24, 28, 30, and 1 Timothy 6:17). But we tend to turn those gifts into idols. Let's not waste our days pursuing things that don't really matter. Let's not spend our lives chasing things that would cause God to say to us what He said to the rich man in 12:20, "Thou fool, this night thy soul shall be required of thee: then whose shall those things be, which thou hast provided?"

Let's determine to invest our time, talents, and treasure in that which has heavenly value (12:34) so we might be "rich toward God" (12:21). This world knows nothing about that, but those of us who are privileged to be part of God's kingdom ought to become experts at it.

Dear Lord, my heart is often captured by the temporal, material pleasures of this world. Please give me the lenses to look at this world with an eternal perspective. May I invest my life and resources in Your Kingdom, in the souls of people who are precious to You, and in that which impacts eternity.

"And he said unto them, Take heed, and beware of covetousness: for a man's life consisteth not in the abundance of the things which he possesseth."

Luke 12:15

DAY 19

LUKE 13–15

God's High Priority of Rescuing the Wounded and Lost

OVERVIEW

Chapters 13 and 14 both include a story of the healing of a precious soul on the Sabbath. To the hypocritical leaders at the Temple, following their man-made regulations concerning the Sabbath was more important than relieving the suffering of one individual. These encounters create an opportunity for Jesus to present several parables concerning the Kingdom of God (chapters 13–14) and the *priority* of God, which is rescuing the lost (chapter 15). People begin to discover that the Kingdom Jesus came to bring is far different from the house of cards constructed by the existing religious leaders.

APPLICATION

The religious leaders of Jesus' day thought that their pomp, polish, and piety would garner the favor of God. They had constructed elaborate regulations and engaged in carefully planned ceremonies to "establish their own righteousness" (Romans 10:3).

But they missed the point. All men are sinners. Everyone is broken. Their religious activity was like lipstick on a pig—and God wasn't impressed (Isaiah 64:6). We are all hopelessly lost and in danger of God's judgment (13:2–5). Only those willing to admit that will receive God's forgiveness and eternal life.

God wasn't looking for people who were good enough to earn His Kingdom. He was looking for people who realized they had no hope of ever being good enough, who would fall down at His feet for mercy. Those would be the ones He would redeem, transform, and make the objects of His eternal pleasure and grace.

It surprised—even enraged—the religious elite that Jesus was more drawn to the "poor, maimed, halt, and blind" and those from the "highways and hedges" than to them (14:21–24). Their pride was wounded. And in their eyes, there was no way He could truly be the Messiah.

These supposed religious leaders were far from God's heart. God's heart is best seen in the shepherd who rejoices over the sheep he has rescued, in the woman who is relieved that her precious treasure is reclaimed, and in the father whose beloved son has finally come home from his wandering (chapter 15).

That's the heart of God. And because it is, you and I (the misfits, outcasts, and rebels) are invited to His table. Aren't you thankful? And don't you want to be a messenger of that good news to others today?

Lord Jesus, thank You being interested in people like me. I'm thankful that You're not impressed by religious pedigree or ceremony, because I could never hope to impress You. I know I fall short and I rejoice over the fact that You saved me. Please point me today in the direction of others, with whom I can share Your love. Reproduce Your heart for the fallen and broken in me, I pray.

"I say unto you, that likewise joy shall be in heaven over one sinner that repenteth, more than over ninety and nine just persons, which need no repentance."

Luke 15:7

DAY 20

LUKE 16–18

The Qualifications and Character of Those in the Kingdom

OVERVIEW

Chapters 16–18 are comprised almost entirely of Jesus' words. He gives five lengthy parables to help His listeners understand how the Kingdom of God functions. He shares the all-important story of the rich man and the beggar Lazarus, both of whom entered eternity—one to Heaven and the other to a tragic place of suffering called Hell. Jesus again confronts the Pharisees (16:15 and 18:10–14) and predicts His death and resurrection (18:31–33). He also heals ten lepers (17:12–19) and one blind beggar (18:35–43).

APPLICATION

What is it that you're praying for? Is there a concern in your life or a breakthrough needed in some relationship or difficulty? I can't know exactly what God's will is concerning the outcome of the burden you're carrying. But I can assure you of one thing: your loving Father wants you to take it to Him in prayer. And He wants you to take it *continually.*

It is impossible to pray too much about a situation. When it comes to God's invitation for you to come to Him in prayer, you cannot outwear your welcome. He won't grow weary with your asking. He told His disciples that "men ought always to pray, and not to faint." In other words, don't grow discouraged while you wait for God to answer. Just keep asking (1 Thessalonians 5:17). As it has often been said, "God's delays are not God's denials."

Jesus gave a parable that went something like this: "If an unscrupulous judge will respond to the repeated requests of a widow who comes seeking justice, God will certainly respond to the repeated requests of His children, in His time."

God answers all of our prayers. Sometimes His answer is "yes" and sometimes it's "no," based on His wisdom and goodness. Other times His answer is "not yet," or "I have something better in mind." But *He always answers*. So keep asking. Because if there's one thing we don't want said of us, it's, "ye have not, because ye ask not" (James 4:2).

Lord, forgive me for neglecting to take my concerns to You in prayer and worrying over them instead. Thank You for Your willingness to patiently hear my requests and bear my burdens. Thank You for giving me Your ear, as a result of first giving me Yourself on the cross. And now, Lord, I come to You with the following requests...

"And he spake a parable unto them to this end, that men ought always to pray, and not to faint;"

Luke 18:1

DAY 21

LUKE 19–21

Jesus at the Temple, Sharing Parables and Prophecies, and Preaching the Gospel

OVERVIEW

Because Luke's Gospel is the most detailed of the four, he includes accounts that the other writers do not, like the wonderful story of Zacchaeus' conversion. After this took place and after one more parable, Jesus triumphantly enters Jerusalem for the final days of His earthly ministry. He drives out the scamming salesmen from the Temple. He demonstrates His wisdom during clashes with the priests, scribes, and Pharisees, and He predicts the coming destruction of Jerusalem.

APPLICATION

I simply love the way the closing verses of Luke 19 (45–48) describe our Lord. Picture it: He enters the Temple, fully in charge. To the religious elite, He is an outsider. But He owns the place—literally. He sweeps out from the temple courts those who are using the worship system to make a quick buck. He scratches off a spot and begins teaching daily in the public square of the Temple as crowds gather. In the background, the befuddled priests and religious bureaucrats wring their hands over the dilemma of this magnetic, miracle–working prophet, whose popularity threatens their power structure. But they're short on ideas because "the people were very attentive to hear him."

Don't we have an amazing, wonderful Saviour? He has ultimate power, absolute authority, and infinite wisdom. To say that He is larger than life is an extraordinary understatement. He is the author and source of life—Creator God in human flesh, teaching and healing on the streets of Jerusalem.

But there's another side to our Saviour that's equally encouraging, and it's seen in the *opening verses* of chapter 19 (1–10), in the story of Zacchaeus. While Jesus attracts crowds, He cares about individuals—even the corrupted ones. Zacchaeus was a publican (think of a tax auditor who extorts people), yet Jesus reached out to him. He knows each of our names, where to find us, and He initiates a friendship with us in spite of who we are, based entirely on His grace. He sees value in those whom others only view with contempt. What a Saviour!

Lord Jesus, I praise You for Your authority, not only over the religious leaders of the first century, but over every authority that ever has been or ever will be. I bow my heart and head before You, humbled and grateful. Use me, I pray, as Your ambassador to the world, to advance Your Kingdom and glorify Your name.

"For the Son of man is come to seek and to save that which was lost."

Luke 19:10

DAY 22

LUKE 22–24

Jesus' Suffering on and Triumph over the Cross of Calvary

OVERVIEW

Jesus shares a meaningful passover meal with His disciples then agonizes in prayer in the Garden of Gethsemane. There, He is arrested and led through four scenes of a mock trial that extends through the night and into the following morning. He is interrogated at the chief priest's palace, then taken to Pilate for questioning, sent to Herod (Pilate's colleague in the Roman government) for interrogation, and finally sent to Pilate. At the Jewish mob's insistent cry, "Crucify him," Pilate has Jesus escorted to Calvary where He is crucified. After His death, He is buried and rises from the grave three days later. He meets with His disciples over a period of forty days and ascends back to Heaven.

APPLICATION

The purpose of the Lord's Table traces back to where today's passage (22:8–20) begins—the upper room where Christ shared His last meal with the disciples before the cross. Jesus instructed the disciples to receive the bread and the cup "in remembrance of me."

The early church continued this ordinance to reflect on the awesome sacrifice Jesus made for them. Paul said, "For as often as ye eat this bread, and drink this cup, ye do shew the Lord's death till he come" (1 Corinthians 11:26). When we gather to observe this ordinance of our Lord, it's an opportunity to do the following:

- To reflect on Christ's love—that He was willing to suffer our shame and bear our guilt.
- To examine our lives—to see if there is anything between us and our Saviour (1 Corinthians 11:28).
- To rededicate ourselves—to living obediently for His glory and pleasure.

Notice the language Jesus used: "This is my body which is *given for you*...This cup is...my blood...which is *shed for you*" (italics mine). Jesus wanted His disciples to take His death *personally*. He wants you to as well. He died for *you*—on your behalf. Individually. Personally. Lovingly. Purposefully.

Ephesians 5:2 says it this way, "And walk in love, as Christ also hath loved us, and hath given himself for us an offering and a sacrifice to God for a sweetsmelling savour."

Lord Jesus, I can never thank You enough for enduring the cross on my behalf. Thank You for Your willingness to suffer and bleed and allow Your body to be broken to forgive me. Thank You for taking the guilt, shame, and pain of my sin in Your very own body on that cross. I praise You for Your love and Your power gloriously demonstrated when you rose from the grave! May I live for You today in a way that reflects Your love, grace, and joy in my life.

"And he took bread, and gave thanks, and brake it, and gave unto them, saying, This is my body which is given for you: this do in remembrance of me."

Luke 22:19

DAY 23

JOHN 1–3

Jesus, the Eternal Word, Is Made Flesh and Dwells among Mankind

OVERVIEW

Among the disciples, the apostle John seems to have had the closest relationship with Jesus. His Gospel record, like Mark's, skips Jesus' birth and childhood, covering only His public ministry—the final three years of His earthly journey. John's Gospel gives extra evidence and emphasis to the deity of Jesus Christ—that He is eternally existent, co-equal with the Father, and the one and only Son of God. After describing the nature of the incarnation in the opening fourteen verses, John presents the ministry of John the Baptist, the introducing of the first few disciples to Jesus, our Lord's first miracle, and Jesus' encounter with Nicodemus.

APPLICATION

All who know Jesus have one thing in common—they were introduced to Him by someone else. The great apostle Peter was no exception. John 1:40–42 records the scene.

Peter's brother Andrew was a disciple of John the Baptist. As a result of John the Baptist's ministry, Andrew began to listen to Jesus teach and concluded that He was indeed the long-awaited Messiah whom the Jewish prophets had foretold. Andrew was so excited about his discovery that he quickly informed his brother Peter proclaiming, "We have found the Messiah." And "he brought him to Jesus" (1:42).

Who could you bring to Jesus? Who could you introduce to Christ? There are people within your sphere of influence—coworkers, neighbors, friends, relatives—whose "relational link" to Jesus could be you! Make no mistake, the Lord intends to use you to bring others to Him.

We tend to fear that those we speak to about Jesus will respond negatively. But if we have truly met Jesus, as Andrew did, we cannot stay silent. And sure, some may respond negatively, but others will respond positively. (You are living proof of that.) And if we tell no one, we have failed without even trying.

Don't sell yourself short. You are probably further along in your spiritual journey, right now, than Andrew was on his when he brought his brother to Jesus. All you have to know is that you have met Jesus and that you want others to know Him too. And then simply tell them who you found.

Lord Jesus, I'm grateful to know You. Like Andrew who was excited about discovering who You are—the Son of God—I, too, am thankful to know You personally. Please use me, as You did him, to bring others and introduce them to You. You are worthy of being shared. And I commit myself to being Your witness today.

"He first findeth his own brother Simon, and saith unto him, We have found the Messias, which is, being interpreted, the Christ. And he brought him to Jesus...."

John 1:41–42

DAY 24

JOHN 4–6

Jesus Presents Himself as the Living Water and Bread of Life

OVERVIEW

John's Gospel contains several of Jesus' stories and sayings that are not contained in the other three Gospels. So our journey through John fills in much of what occurred "between the lines" of Matthew, Mark, and Luke. And it's powerful! In John 4–6, Jesus encounters a woman whose life is transformed from adulteress to evangelist in a single day. Jesus then heals the nobleman's son and a man who'd been crippled for thirty-eight years. This healing occurs on the Sabbath, which sparks a confrontation with the Jewish leaders in which Jesus plainly explains that He is the Son of God. Later, He feeds the five thousand and explains His role as the bread of life sent from Heaven.

APPLICATION

Most people have enough religion to make them dangerous. The Samaritan woman at the well, for example, tried to initiate a debate with Jesus about the proper historical location for worship. Then, the "Sabbath police" demonstrated that they cared more about compliance with their man-made rules than the miraculous healing of a man.

Jesus cut through the religious confusion and superstition with a simple message: as the Son of God, only through faith in Him could a man have a relationship with the Father and obtain eternal life. He expressed this repeatedly in today's reading (4:14; 5:18, 24, 39–44; 6:35, 47, 51).

Jesus made it clear that He wasn't just another prophet. He was the living water, the bread of life, the one and only way to God. A line in the sand had been drawn—His listeners must either accept or reject it. Either believe Him, receive Him, and forsake their previous religious ties; or turn away. When faced with this choice, "many...went back and walked no more with him" (6:66).

Jesus turned to the disciples and asked, "Will ye also go away?" Peter's reaction is classic: "To whom shall we go?" Then he said the most important thing anyone could ever say: "And we believe and are sure that thou art that Christ, the Son of the living God" (6:69).

All who come to that right conclusion about Jesus, from that day until now, and call on Him for salvation are immediately accepted into a relationship with God—as if they'd taken a drink of living water or eaten the bread of life.

Have you made that decision? If so, have you thanked Jesus lately for what He has provided you? Have you shared it—the most important truth in the world—with someone recently?

Lord Jesus, I'd like to express the sentiment of Peter. I believe You. I'm sure You are who You said You are—the very Son of God. I praise You for this, I thank You for coming, and I'm trusting You for my soul's salvation. Thank You for making salvation simple. Thank You for doing the hard part, by allowing Your body to be broken like bread. Thank You for sharing Your life so I can have eternal life.

"Verily, verily, I say unto you, He that heareth my word, and believeth on him that sent me, hath everlasting life, and shall not come into condemnation; but is passed from death unto life."

John 5:24

DAY 25

JOHN 7–9

Jesus Exonerates a Woman, Confronts the Pharisees, and Opens Blind Eyes

OVERVIEW

Jesus travels from Galilee down to Jerusalem for the Feast of Tabernacles, an annual pilgrimage to the Temple for faithful Jews. He teaches in the Temple while common people and religious leaders both debate over what to make of Him. When Jesus refuses to condemn a woman to death with the Scribes and Pharisees, it leads to an intense confrontation between Him and the religious ruling class. Then, they are further enraged when Jesus heals a blind man on the Sabbath day.

APPLICATION

Opinions about Jesus swirled around Jerusalem. Many believed on Him after hearing His words and witnessing His miracles. No doubt the Holy Spirit was involved in convincing their hearts. But many others did not come to that conclusion.

There were debaters, who deliberated over what town He came from, who He was related to, and where His power originated. There were despisers, who seeing Him as a threat to their authority, sought first to discredit Him and then to destroy Him. And there were the disciples who believed and followed. But the most important things anyone said about Jesus were those He said Himself:

- "He that sent me is true, whom ye know not. But I know him: for I am from him" (7:28–29).
- "If ye had known me, ye should have known my Father also" (8:19).
- "If the Son therefore shall make you free, ye shall be free indeed" (8:36).
- "I proceeded forth and came from God" (8:42).
- "Before Abraham was, I am" (8:58).

These statements clearly established His deity. And because of their clarity, the Jewish leaders labeled Him a blasphemer (10:33), ultimately demanding His execution.

But there's one more statement He made in today's reading that I just love: "And he that sent me is with me: the Father hath not left me alone; for I do always those things that please him" (John 8:29). This provides a great pattern for us to follow:

- Jesus advanced the Father's purpose.
- Jesus experienced the Father's presence.
- Jesus lived for the Father's pleasure.

Let's make that verse our motto today.

Father, thank You that, just as You sent Jesus to earth, You have also sent me (John 20:21) on a mission as Your child and servant. Please use me to advance Your purposes in this world today. Thank You for sharing Your presence with me by Your indwelling Holy Spirit. What a treasure! My heart's desire today, Lord, is to please and glorify You.

"And he that sent me is with me: the Father hath not left me alone; for I do always those things that please him."

John 8:29

DAY 26

JOHN 10–12

Jesus Demonstrates His Authority over Death and the Grave

OVERVIEW

Jesus had already presented Himself as the living water, the bread of life, and the light of the world. Now He presents Himself as the good shepherd in chapter 10 and the resurrection and the life in chapter 11 just before calling His friend Lazarus out of the grave. In chapter 12 Jesus enjoys a meal with the recently-raised Lazarus and his two sisters, then enters Jerusalem for the final time, where public opinions swirl and confrontations escalate with the Jewish establishment.

APPLICATION

The account of Lazarus' resurrection has implications for so many areas of our lives, both in time and eternity. It's an enjoyable narrative, as we observe our Lord's empathy toward His friends (11:33–35). It deals with death and disappointment—realities for us all.

Early in the passage, we read, "Now Jesus loved Martha, and her sister [Mary], and Lazarus" (11:5). Don't ever forget, during your time of difficulty, this simple fact: Jesus loves you. Nothing He does or (as in this case) does *not* do in your life negates His love.

Jesus didn't rush to the rescue. He sometimes does. But not this time. He waited in the outskirts of Judaea a number of days before arriving on the scene. But though He wasn't present physically, He was fully aware of and had a plan for the situation. He said to the disciples, "And I am glad for your sakes that I was not there, to the intent ye may believe" (11:15). When you're not sure where God is in a situation, rest in knowing that He's still in control.

When Jesus arrived in Bethany, where Lazarus lived, He comforted Martha and Mary with what they already knew about Him—that He was the resurrection and the life (11:25). That's what we all need: first His presence, and second reminders (prompted by the Spirit) of what we already know to be true about Him. He's good. He's sovereign. He's wise. And He's at work.

Then twice Jesus emphasized to Martha the importance of her own faith. After expressing His ability to give eternal life, He said, "Believest thou this?" (11:26) Then, a few moments later, "Said I not unto thee, that, if thou wouldest believe, thou shouldest see the glory of God?" (11:40).

So yes, God's power, love, and truth are key elements in working difficulty together for your good. But your faith is also a key element. So during those moments of difficulty, be reminded of Jesus' message to Martha: If you believe, you'll see the glory of God.

Lord Jesus, I believe in Your goodness, Your love, and Your power. Thank You that when I am dealing with disappointment—or even death—that You are very much present and in control. I trust You, and I thank You for loving me and for sharing Your resurrection power with me.

"Jesus said unto her, I am the resurrection, and the life: he that believeth in me, though he were dead, yet shall he live: And whosoever liveth and believeth in me shall never die. Believest thou this?"

John 11:25–26

DAY 27

JOHN 13–15

Jesus Describes His Impending Departure and the Coming Comforter

OVERVIEW

Today's passage records the events and conversations that took place between Christ and His disciples in the final hours before His arrest. Though all four Gospel writers describe the sharing of the passover meal in the upper room, John is the only writer who includes the detail of Jesus washing the disciples' feet—an extraordinary act of humility. Then, after predicting Judas' betrayal and Peter's denial, Jesus enters a series of conversations about the future (chapters 14–16), which begin in the upper room and continue as they make their way to Gethsemane.

APPLICATION

The opportunity to listen in on Jesus' conversations with His disciples during the final hours of His earthly ministry before Calvary is significant and instructive.

First, Jesus shares some sobering news: "I go away" (14:28). The disciples had forsaken all to follow Him. And now, just three years into their relationship, He's leaving? Jesus had been preparing for this all along, and on multiple occasions He had tried to tell His disciples. But it was unwelcome news to them, and it seems this was the first time they began to grasp that He really was about to be crucified.

Jesus knew also that in the coming days life would become difficult as the disciples carried the baton of leadership in the early church. Thus He warned them, "If the world hate you, ye know that it hated me before it hated you…If they have persecuted me, they will also persecute you" (15:18–20). But Jesus explained, "Let not your heart be troubled" because "I will come again" (14:1–3).

Not only would Jesus Himself return, but in the meantime He would send the Comforter (14:26), the Holy Spirit, who would literally be *God's presence* in the life of all believers. This way He could be with every believer at all times, instead of being limited by a human body. Jesus and His Father would make their "abode" (home) in every believer (14:23).

In chapter 15, Jesus explained that the disciples' (and our) relationship with Him would be an abiding arrangement in which we are connected to Him like branches to a life-giving vine.

But the decision to abide is ours. We get to determine the strength of the connection between us and Christ each day, by whether we spend time with Him in prayer and Scripture meditation and by whether we keep the pathway clear through confessing and forsaking sin. Abiding in Him will lead to personal fruitfulness (v. 5), love (v. 10), joy (v. 11), answered prayer (vv. 7, 16), and friendship with Him (v. 15).

Lord Jesus, thank You for calling me Your friend, and for being the great life-giving, fruit-producing vine to whom I have the privilege of being connected each day. Thank You for sending Your Holy Spirit to abide within my life. I yield myself to You today. I ask You to fill me, guide me, empower me, and use me. Please produce fruit in my life today in a way that will glorify and please You.

"Abide in me, and I in you. As the branch cannot bear fruit of itself, except it abide in the vine; no more can ye, except ye abide in me. I am the vine, ye are the branches: He that abideth in me, and I in him, the same bringeth forth much fruit: for without me ye can do nothing."

John 15:4–5

DAY 28

JOHN 16–18

Jesus Prepares and Prays for His Disciples Before His Arrest

OVERVIEW

Chapter 16 continues the conversation Jesus began in chapter 14 with His disciples concerning His coming departure. He assures them that His departure is in their best interest, as the Comforter will guide, teach, and accompany them. We then read the lengthiest recorded prayer of our Lord, providing us a glimpse into His tender relationship with the Father as well as His heart for His followers. Finally, He is arrested and brought before former priest, Annas, current high priest, Caiaphas, and then the Roman governor, Pilate.

APPLICATION

It must have been an amazing thing to personally hear the prayers of Jesus as the disciples did. I am thankful that His prayer recorded in John 17 has been preserved in God's Word for us to read today.

Jesus expresses His unity with and longing for His Father in Heaven. But the majority of His prayer involves intercession for His disciples. Not just His first twelve disciples, but all who would eventually follow Him: "Neither pray I for these alone, but for them also which shall believe on me through their word;" (17:20). Jesus prayed for you and me!

Jesus prayed for the Father's protection in our lives (17:15–17). We live in a broken and sin-sick world, and Jesus does not want us to become infected by it. We don't belong to this world. We belong to His world—His kingdom. So we must pursue sanctification by God's truth.

He also prays for our unity. "That they all may be one…that they also may be one in us" (17:21). Are you working toward unity with your brothers and sisters in Christ?

In your own family? In your church? United we stand; divided we fall. Jesus knew that. Your pursuit of unity is the answer to Jesus' prayers.

And He prayed that we could be used in leading others to Him. "…that the world may believe that thou hast sent me" (17:21, 23). He prayed that, as a result of our union with each other and with Him, others would come to know Him. Are you seeking to be a part of the answer to that?

Lord Jesus, thank You for praying for me. I pray along with You. Please keep me from becoming infected by this world. Sanctify me by Your truth. Clean me, transform me, and make me more like You. Help me to function in unity with my brothers and sisters in Your family. And then use us together to help people in this world know who You are and how You came to save them.

"I pray not that thou shouldest take them out of the world, but that thou shouldest keep them from the evil. They are not of the world, even as I am not of the world. Sanctify them through thy truth: thy word is truth."

John 17:15–17

DAY 29

JOHN 19–21

Jesus Is Crucified and Risen, Then Deputizes His Disciples to Carry On His Work

OVERVIEW

It is appropriate that the apostle John includes several details in his account of the crucifixion and resurrection that pertain to him personally. He describes how Jesus spoke to Mary from the cross and bequeathed her care to him. He describes what it was like for him and Peter to race to the tomb and find it empty, just as Mary Magdalene had said it was. Finally, he reviews the time when Jesus called him and Peter to once again leave their fishing and serve His cause, once and for all.

APPLICATION

The disciples were bewildered, in a fog about the future, even though Jesus had risen from the grave. They didn't know that they would help launch an institution not yet understood in their minds, but that would become God's chief work on earth over the coming two millennia—the institution of the local church.

Peter said, "I go a fishing" (21:3) to which the six other disciples with him replied, "We also go with thee." They simply didn't know what to do next. But then Jesus met them and expressed His intentions for using them in His kingdom. In just a few weeks, Peter would preach the gospel and three thousand people would be saved (Acts 2:41). Then thousands more.

This conversation on the Sea of Galilee, one of the Lord's final meetings with the disciples, would help prepare Peter for God's mighty purpose for his life. And it's instructive for us.

Peter needed to decide whether the Lord was his chief love or just one of his many interests, like fishing, for example. So Jesus asked Peter—three times—whether he loved Jesus supremely. Settling this issue was critical because of what Peter would face in the coming days.

Peter also needed to overcome the tendency all the disciples had (one we still have), to compare himself and his assignments, requirements, and challenges to his fellow laborers. When Jesus, in essence, told Peter he would die a martyr's death, he replied, "Lord, and what shall this man [John] do?" (21:21). Jesus' answer is classic. And it's great advice for Christian servants today: "What is that to thee? follow thou me."

If God will use us, as He ultimately used Peter, He must first call us to unwavering love for Him above all else *and* an abandoning of our tendency to be distracted by others. It's all about Him. Not us. Not them. *Him*—His cause, His Name, His glory, His purposes, His kingdom. And it's a privilege to be involved.

Lord Jesus, I recognize Your last words to Peter were similar to Your first words, "Follow me." And that's really the essence of what I need to do. Help me to follow You today and in the days ahead. I want to walk in Your steps, obey Your Word, and follow Your leadership day by day. I trust You to use me as I follow. And, Lord, I love You. May I love You even more.

"So when they had dined, Jesus saith to Simon Peter, Simon, son of Jonas, lovest thou me more than these? He saith unto him, Yea, Lord; thou knowest that I love thee. He saith unto him, Feed my lambs."

John 21:15

DAY 30

ACTS 1–3

After Jesus Ascends, the Spirit Descends and Empowers the Apostles for Ministry

OVERVIEW

We've just finished the Gospels—the four overlapping biographical records of Christ's earthly ministry. Acts opens up where each of those Gospels leave off, in the days between the resurrection of Christ and His ascension back to Heaven (a period of forty days). In chapter 2, Jesus' promise is fulfilled as the Holy Spirit arrives to indwell the disciples, empowering them for ministry. Then Peter preached, and three thousand people are saved and baptized. Those believers begin their growth journey, and Peter is given yet another opportunity to preach the gospel to a large crowd after healing a lame man at the Temple.

Acts is the most thoroughly historical book in the New Testament, as it records the approximately thirty years of church history that immediately followed Christ. It follows the spread of the gospel from Jerusalem outward, across the Roman empire.

APPLICATION

The church described in Acts 2 was in its infancy. It had started, in essence, with Jesus and His disciples. This little group of quiet believers were meeting and waiting, almost secretively at first. Then, as the Day of Pentecost arrived and (more importantly) the Holy Spirit arrived, Peter preached, and the first great multitude of souls were converted and added to the church.

In the verses following (2:41–47), we get a view into the first church that provides an extraordinary pattern for all of us who serve in churches today. In this church, there was instruction (2:42). People were learning the doctrines of the apostles which Jesus had given. They read and studied and discussed what Jesus had taught them (Matthew 28:20).

In this church, there was unity and interdependence (2:44–46). People rallied around one another, meeting needs, and bearing burdens. There was camaraderie as they spent time together praying, studying, and sharing meals.

There was joy (2:46–47). These people were glad to be saved! They were thankful to have received the truth about Jesus Christ. They laughed and created memories together, forging bonds that would extend into eternity.

There was a passion for those outside the church, who needed Christ (2:47). They gained favor in those people's eyes through their faithful living and witnessing. And God continued to add new people to their assembly in spite of their complete lack of experience, financial resources, buildings, programs, or technology.

What an example they are for us! Are you part of a local church? If so, I hope you're helping that church resemble the first-century church, which impacted its world for Christ in an extraordinary way.

Father, thank You for sending Your Holy Spirit to empower and use the disciples. But even more, thank You for sending Him to empower and accompany me. I pray that You'll use me, as You did those first disciples, to share the gospel with others. And help me be a part of making our church all it can be by living out the biblical responsibilities we have been given.

"And they, continuing daily with one accord in the temple, and breaking bread from house to house, did eat their meat with gladness and singleness of heart, Praising God, and having favour with all the people. And the Lord added to the church daily such as should be saved."

Acts 2:46–47

DAY 31

ACTS 4–6

The Church's First Generation of Believers Fearlessly Witness for Christ

OVERVIEW

Twice in today's passage the disciples are arrested by the Jewish rulers and ordered to cease and desist their preaching about Christ's resurrection. But both times the disciples courageously continue their work. As the church members seek to meet one another's needs through sacrificial offerings, one couple lies to the apostles about the amount of an offering they had given, trying to take credit for generosity they did not actually practice. They lost their lives in a rare but sobering account of how seriously God values integrity. In chapter 6, the apostles discern the need for delegation, and so they select seven godly men to assist them in serving their burgeoning congregation in Jerusalem, now comprised of several thousand members.

APPLICATION

Upon the healing of the lame man at the Temple, the religious rulers did not appreciate that thousands had gathered to hear the gospel of Christ—a message they were unsuccessfully attempting to silence. So they arrested, threatened, and released the disciples. The disciples' zeal would not be quenched, however, and their voices would not be silenced. Peter said, "For we cannot but speak the things which we have seen and heard" (4:20). So they gathered with their fellow believers, prayed for boldness and power, and continued witnessing.

Chapter 5 records their second arrest. Only this time, it was an angel from Heaven who came and released them from prison. Imagine the surprise of the priests when in the morning, as they planned to interrogate the disciples, they heard reports that they were already preaching in the temple square! Peter again spoke for the group, "We ought to obey God rather than men" (5:29).

This time they beat the disciples and commanded them yet again to keep silent. It's humbling and inspiring to read their reaction: "And they departed from the presence of the council, rejoicing that they were counted worthy to suffer shame for his name. And daily in the temple, and in every house, they ceased not to teach and preach Jesus Christ" (5:41–42).

These courageous Christians could not keep quiet. They were so overwhelmed by the reality of Jesus Christ, His incarnation, His work on the Cross, and His resurrection, that they saw only one option—tell everyone they possibly could, by every means possible, who Jesus was and about the salvation He offered.

How convinced are we? How personal and real is Christ's work to us? May God ignite the courage and boldness in us that He did in them to faithfully witness of His dear Son!

Father, forgive me for not witnessing to the people around me with the same boldness, courage, and faithfulness as the disciples. The truth is, the reality of the gospel hasn't changed. Your Spirit's ability to empower us hasn't changed. Your love for people's souls hasn't changed. I get focused on insignificant matters when all around me there are people who need to know about Your Son. Use me as Your witness, I pray.

"And daily in the temple, and in every house, they ceased not to teach and preach Jesus Christ."

Acts 5:42

DAY 32

ACTS 7–9

Stephen Preaches to a Council, Philip Preaches in Samaria, and Paul Is Converted on His Way to Damascus

OVERVIEW

Today's passage covers *a lot* of ground. It contains some accounts very important to the future of the church. Stephen becomes the church's first martyr. His sermon reviews the flawed history of the Jewish nation, climaxing in the crucifixion of their Messiah. Philip is the first to carry the gospel outside of Jerusalem, taking the message to Samaria with great results and even further to the Ethiopian man in the desert. In chapter 9, the single greatest turning point in Acts occurs when *Saul*, the persecutor of the church, is converted and transformed into *Paul*, the preacher of the gospel.

APPLICATION

Saul had been the greatest human threat to the church's mission. He was a leading agent in the Jewish leaders' strategy to stop the spread of the gospel. But he was converted and became the greatest catalyst for the church's mission. This required the supernatural intervention of God in his life (9:5). But there's more to it than that.

The case of Saul the persecutor turned Paul the missionary includes a component still present today when people's lives are transformed—that is, faithful believers whom God can use to touch others' lives. We see this in how God used Stephen's testimony to impact Saul. When Stephen was executed, the perpetrators handed their coats to young Saul (7:58) who was "consenting unto his death" (8:1). What an impression Stephen's faith made on the religious zealot. In fact, Paul himself later bore testimony to Stephen's impact (22:20).

But surely God used other Christians, too. Saul broke down people's doors, hauling them off to jail for their worship of Jesus (8:3). He "breathed out threatenings" like a dragon (9:1). But these simple, sincere people were unflappable. And Saul was impressed.

Later, God used Ananias to come alongside Paul immediately upon his conversion. He was the first Christian to call him, "Brother Saul" (9:17), offering acceptance, grace, and guidance. Then God used Barnabas to introduce Paul to the apostles (9:27).

Before, during, and after Saul's conversion, various faithful Christians simply did their part, not knowing how their faithfulness fit into the larger plan of God.

You and I don't know whose lives our simple faithfulness is impacting today. Our endurance in trials, our encouraging words, our courageous witness, our loving acceptance, our teaching and mentoring—all of these work together, by the grace and providence of God to impact lives for eternity.

Lord, use me in the lives of others, I pray. I rejoice to consider that You may use someone I influence to advance Your cause to an even greater degree than You use me. Make me an encouragement. Help me be a faithful testimony. Use my witness. I thank You for including my simple, imperfect efforts in Your work in people's lives.

"And Ananias went his way, and entered into the house; and putting his hands on him said, Brother Saul, the Lord, even Jesus, that appeared unto thee in the way as thou camest, hath sent me, that thou mightest receive thy sight, and be filled with the Holy Ghost."

Acts 9:17

DAY 33

ACTS 10–12

Peter Takes the Gospel to the Gentiles and Is Miraculously Delivered from Prison

OVERVIEW

Up until Acts 10, nearly all those who had received Christ were Jews. But in chapter 10, Peter discovers that God's plan of salvation through Jesus is for all nations when God sends him to the seeking Gentile, Cornelius. Then, in chapter 11, the gospel is carried by other faithful witnesses to Antioch, where more Gentiles believe on Christ. In chapter 12, Peter faces execution. But we see the power of a praying church as he is released from prison by an angel at night, during the very hours the church was praying for him.

APPLICATION

The Bible records of Barnabas, "He was a good man" (11:24). What a simple yet profoundly important description! Every church I'm familiar with needs more good men and women. What prompted God to call Barnabas "a good man"?

- He was accepting. The believers in Antioch were among the first Gentile converts. Instead of looking down on them as some in Jerusalem did (11:2), he joyfully welcomed them to the family of God (11:23). He had done the same for Paul (9:27).
- He was an encourager. The disciples actually nicknamed him Barnabas (his given name was Joses) because it means "encourager" (4:36). Today's passage says he "exhorted" the new believers in Antioch (11:23).
- He was a mentor. He challenged the converts in Antioch to "cleave unto the Lord" (11:23), and spent an entire year helping to ground them in their faith (11:26).

- He was Spirit-filled (11:24). Barnabas walked with God in prayer and study, seeking the leadership and guidance of God's Spirit.
- He was generous. He sold land, donating the funds to meet the needs of struggling new believers who had been displaced from their homes in distant places (4:37).
- He was a witness. One result of his arrival in Antioch was that "much people was added unto the Lord" (11:24).

Which of these areas come more naturally to you? Which do you need to work on, in your attempt to be a truly *good* man or woman for the glory of God and for the advancement of His purposes? Let's make these traits our target.

Lord, I thank You that I don't have to earn Your acceptance, by my works. I have received the righteousness of Your Son, Jesus, applied to my life, so that when You see me You only see the good record of Christ. But You also know that I have a desire to practice goodness as a believer so that I might be a blessing to others. I'm a work in progress in that regard. So please give me the opportunities and the enabling required to encourage, bless, and help others today as Barnabas did in his day.

"For he was a good man, and full of the Holy Ghost and of faith: and much people was added unto the Lord."

Acts 11:24

DAY 34

ACTS 13–15

Paul's First Missionary Journey and the Jerusalem Council

OVERVIEW

At chapter 13, halfway through the book of Acts, the narrative shifts from focusing mostly on Peter and the ministry surrounding Jerusalem, to Paul and the ministry spreading from Antioch. Chapter 13 opens with a young but healthy congregation in Antioch-Syria that deputizes two of its key workers as missionaries to reach people in new regions. Chapters 13 and 14 record Paul's first missionary journey as he and Barnabas share the gospel on Cyprus, then in Antioch-Pisidia, Iconium, Lystra, and Derbe. In chapter 15, Paul and Barnabas travel to Jerusalem to participate in a meeting to clarify the apostles' position on whether Gentile believers are required to adhere to historic Jewish religious customs.

APPLICATION

Evangelistic missions is the heart of God! And today's passage gives us a fantastic pattern for biblical missions. It is churches sending godly men (13:3) with the gospel to places where people do not know God. It is faithful Christians who endure hardship (14:19–20) to lead people to Christ, plant churches, and invest in lives. It's discipleship, where new converts are taught the Word (14:22). It is churches supporting missionaries along the way, making their work possible financially (15:3). It is reporting back to those sending churches what God has accomplished through the missionaries (14:27). And it is doing these things all over again (15:40).

All of us have a role to play when it comes to missions. We can pray regularly, by name, for missionaries we know. We can pray for specific people groups who need the Lord. We can host missionaries in our churches and homes and stay in contact with them while they're on the field. (They're real-life heroes!) We can participate in mission trips, where we can be involved on the ground, reaching people for the Lord.

We can give financially to help get more missionaries to more fields more quickly. And some of us should *go*, as full-time missionaries, to distant places with the gospel.

In 1956, Jim Elliot, Nate Saint, and three other missionaries were tragically martyred as they sought to deliver the gospel to the Auca Indians in Ecuador. During their preparations for their mission, Nate Saint, the team's pilot, made this observation: "People who do not know the Lord ask why in the world we waste our lives as missionaries. They forget that they too are expending their lives…and when the bubble has burst, they will have nothing of eternal significance to show for the years they have wasted."

We learn from the example of Paul, Barnabas, and people like Nate Saint, that the most important thing we can do this side of Heaven is be involved in reaching people with the gospel of Christ. What are you doing to reflect God's heart for missions?

Lord, it is because of missionaries that I have the gospel today. Thank You for calling and using generations of faithful witnesses to get the good news of salvation all the way to me—and to the millions of others around the planet. But Lord, I realize there are many millions, still, who do not know You. We who have the truth have an obligation to do whatever we can to get the gospel to those who don't. Forgive me for my lack of concern. Please use my witness as a part of Your plan to get the gospel to the nations.

"And when they were come, and had gathered the church together, they rehearsed all that God had done with them, and how he had opened the door of faith unto the Gentiles."

Acts 14:27

DAY 35

ACTS 16–18

Paul's Second Missionary Journey Delivers the Gospel to Europe

OVERVIEW

Before Paul's second missionary journey, he and Barnabas parted ways and Silas became his new traveling companion. They set out to visit the churches established on the first journey, then planned on carving out new territory for the gospel. After a brief delay in discerning the Lord's leading, a clear call came in a vision in which Paul saw a man call to him, "Come over into Macedonia, and help us." Paul and his team, which by then included Timothy and Luke (the writer of Acts), immediately crossed the Aegean Sea, taking the gospel for the first time to the continent of Europe, starting in modern-day Greece. The cities where they preached included Philippi, Thessalonica, Berea, Athens, and Corinth.

APPLICATION

Paul was not only the first and greatest missionary in the history of the church, but he was also one of God's servants who endured the greatest suffering. (You can read his inventory of trouble in 2 Corinthians 11:23–28.) In his last letter, he said, "I have fought a good fight" (2 Timothy 4:7). He said Timothy would be required to "endure hardness, as a good soldier" (2:3).

Television evangelists sometimes teach that if we just have enough faith, God will make sure we don't face any trials and will bless us with unlimited health and wealth. These hucksters avoid an extraordinary amount of the New Testament to justify their false teaching.

Jesus Himself said, "In the world ye shall have tribulation...." But what I'd like to emphasize today is how we respond to those difficulties. Because Jesus went on to say, "...but be of good cheer; I have overcome the world" (John 16:33).

How do you tend to respond to trouble? How did Paul respond? Remember, yesterday we read of his being stoned and left for dead in Lystra. In every single city Paul visited, he faced opposition or slander. And for what? For simply following God's call and preaching the good news of Jesus Christ. In today's reading, he is beaten and thrown in jail. How did he and Silas respond? "And at midnight Paul and Silas prayed, and sang praises unto God: and the prisoners heard them" (16:25). They prayed and praised. And in the ensuing moments, they graciously led the very man who had beaten them to the saving knowledge of Jesus Christ. And Philippi became a thriving center of evangelism.

God can use His children in unique and unexpected ways when we respond to trials with grace and poise. The next time we think the whole world is against us and nothing's going our way, remember Paul and Silas. They were falsely accused, beaten, and jailed. And they prayed and praised. You and I can, too.

Lord, forgive me for my tendency to complain. Forgive me for being prone to become discouraged over the smallest difficulties. Jesus, You said, "be of good cheer" because You have overcome the world; but sometimes I act as if the world has overcome me. Thank You that it hasn't. Yes, I have much to pray for, but I also have much to praise You for. I'm thankful that You're good, faithful, loving, wise, and sovereign. And I trust You with the details of my life.

"And at midnight Paul and Silas prayed, and sang praises unto God: and the prisoners heard them."

Acts 16:25

DAY 36

ACTS 19–21

Paul's Third Missionary Journey: Leaving a Legacy in Asia Minor and Europe

OVERVIEW

During Paul's third missionary journey, he retraces his steps through most of the cities where he preached during his first journey, helping to further establish the churches in their faith. Paul is on the move from city to city during this journey, though he spends a larger block of time than usual—two years—in the city of Ephesus. The latter half of chapter 20 records a heart-to-heart meeting between Paul and the leaders of the Ephesian churches before he departs. Paul makes his way back to the home base of Antioch and determines to visit Jerusalem. While there, Paul is nearly killed by a mob of Jews who view him as a religious traitor before a Roman guard arrests him in the scuffle.

APPLICATION

Paul's conversation with the Ephesian elders (20:18–35) provides great instruction and inspiration for any servant of the Lord, whether a volunteer or full-time minister. In this monologue, Paul urges them to care for the flock God has entrusted them. He warns them of opposition. He reviews his own ministry among them as an example. And in the midst of this, there's a great pattern for Christian service found in verse 24.

Paul says that he knows "bonds and afflictions" are coming his way. But, he says, "none of these things move me." In this statement, we see Paul's commitment. He wasn't going to allow adversity to *move* him from God's calling and plan for his life. We are often tempted to allow circumstances to shake and loosen our commitment. But not Paul.

We also see Paul's disposition toward himself. He said, "neither count I my life dear unto myself." Paul had abandoned earthly ambition and temporal gain. He wasn't in it for what he could get out of it. How he was treated or what he received weren't factors in his service to the Lord. Oh, that each of us would become increasingly less important (*dear*) to ourselves!

Finally, in this verse, we see Paul's aim—his vision for his future. He said, "that I might finish my course with joy, and the ministry…to testify the gospel…." Paul just wanted to cross the finish line with joy in his heart—joy produced by knowing he had done his best for his master. The passion of his heart was to know Christ and make him known.

What's your vision for the days ahead—between today and your arrival in Heaven? Why not borrow Paul's? Finish your course with joy, telling people the good news about Jesus Christ.

Lord, may I go the distance as Your immovable servant who lays aside my own concerns and joyfully testifies to others of Your saving grace! This is my prayer and my goal. Please enable me as I seek to follow Paul's example. Forgive me for so often faltering in my commitment or chasing other things. May the passion of my life be testifying the gospel of Your grace!

"But none of these things move me, neither count I my life dear unto myself, so that I might finish my course with joy, and the ministry, which I have received of the Lord Jesus, to testify the gospel of the grace of God."

Acts 20:24

DAY 37

ACTS 22–25

Paul Testifies of Christ to Roman Governors and Audiences

OVERVIEW

Chapter 21 ended with Paul being taken into custody by a Roman centurion due to the ruckus in the Temple. But before being led away, Paul is allowed to say a few words from the exit stairway to the crowd gathered below and, beginning in chapter 22, shares his salvation experience with them. Paul is later transferred from the jail in Jerusalem to the jail in Caesarea to avoid an angry Jewish mob. There, he shares his defense before Governor Felix, followed by Felix's replacement, Governor Festus, and finally, he shares his testimony with regional King Agrippa. The Jews push for his death, as they did with Jesus, and the Roman rulers don't know what to make of it. Paul then requests his case be taken all the way to Caesar's court in Rome.

APPLICATION

The principle of stewardship applies to many areas of life, including opportunities for serving the Lord and witnessing of Christ. Paul was a good steward of his opportunities, so God was able to entrust more occasions to him in making an impact with the gospel message. Paul was unashamed, taking every opportunity to speak out for his Saviour.

He wasn't intimidated by the Jewish religious rulers who wanted him dead. He wasn't frightened by the Roman authorities who held his legal case in their hands and could order his death. Regardless of the audience, he saw them as candidates for receiving the gospel.

During one of his nights in jail, between his public testimonies, the Lord appeared to him, saying "Be of good cheer, Paul: for as thou has testified of me in Jerusalem, so must thou bear witness also at Rome" (23:11).

Paul had long wanted to travel to Rome to preach the gospel but had not yet had the opportunity. Now, though in custody, he was going to get that chance. The Jewish plaintiffs and the Roman rulers were merely pawns in a sovereign God's hand, facilitating the movement of His servant to his next station of service.

God's ways are not our ways. He can take the detours of our lives and turn them into opportunities for usefulness—if we will prove ourselves good stewards of the opportunities we've already been given. So let me ask: What are you doing with the opportunities God has given to share your faith with those in your current sphere of influence?

Let's be faithful stewards of the gospel.

Father, thank You for Your leadership in Paul's life and in my life as well. It's humbling to consider that You intend and desire to use me, just as You used Paul. I know my opportunities will be different from his in size and shape. But nonetheless, they are opportunities to share the same glorious gospel of our great Saviour. So they are significant. Please help me to see and seize opportunities as a faithful steward, witnessing for You.

"And the night following the Lord stood by him, and said, Be of good cheer, Paul: for as thou hast testified of me in Jerusalem, so must thou bear witness also at Rome."

Acts 23:11

DAY 38

ACTS 26–28

Paul's Perilous Journey to Rome

OVERVIEW

Paul, still in the custody of the Romans in Caesarea, shares his salvation testimony with Agrippa, who is "almost persuaded." Then, resulting from his appeal to Caesar, Paul boards a ship with other prisoners to cross the Mediterranean Sea. Their ship is lost to stormy seas, and their lives are nearly lost as well. Upon their arrival in Rome, Paul is placed on house arrest where he is able to encourage believers and witness to Jewish leaders and Roman magistrates.

APPLICATION

The harrowing account of Paul's shipwreck reads like a cliffhanger. All 276 passengers nearly lost their lives but narrowly escaped as the ship ran aground on the tiny island of Malta. Although God protected them and they eventually continued on to Rome, the leaders really should have listened to Paul. He said it himself, as they struggled against the storm: "Sirs, ye should have hearkened unto me, and not have loosed from Crete, and to have gained this harm and loss" (27:21).

Back on the island of Crete, as they stopped in port midway through their journey, he warned them, "Sirs, I perceive that this voyage will be with hurt and much damage, not only of the lading and ship, but also of our lives" (27:10). There are three lessons in this story:

First, the *experts* are often wrong. When Paul warned of trouble, the Roman guard listened to the ship's captain instead of the preacher (27:11). After all, who would know more about weather forecasts at sea? Remember, just because it's what the experts say doesn't mean it's God's way. God's ways often defy conventional, earthly wisdom. That's why following Him requires faith.

Second, the *majority* is often wrong. The centurion and captain listened to the voice of the majority of the passengers and determined to sail on. The majority opinion prevailed (27:12). Our culture is constantly attempting to define and redefine right and wrong. And they have been getting it wrong for generations! God's Word must shape our values, morals, ethics, and character, otherwise we will fall victim to the shifting winds of culture.

Finally, God's sovereignty allows Him to redeem poor decisions, working all things (like the foolish choices of centurions and ship captains) together for the good of His children and the advancement of His purposes. An angel appeared to Paul during the storm, saying, "Fear not, Paul; thou must be brought before Caesar" (27:24).

God is as involved in your situation as He was in Paul's storm at sea. If you're seeking Him and making yourself available to His purposes, He will see you safely through to your destination.

Father, thank You for Your sovereign and providential hand of leadership, guidance, and protection in my life. I praise You that I will never be the final victim of someone else, or even of my own poor choices, because You are over and around all of those things—working them together for my good. Please help me to cooperate with You as You lead me forward to advance Your purposes and glory.

"Wherefore, sirs, be of good cheer: for I believe God, that it shall be even as it was told me."

Acts 27:25

DAY 39

ROMANS 1–3

Case Closed: All Mankind Stands Guilty before God

OVERVIEW

Today's reading takes a major shift. We are moving from historical accounts (the four Gospels and Acts) to *epistles*, or letters. The next thirty-one days will take us through thirteen letters, all written by the apostle Paul. These letters were addressed to churches in seven cities, including several of the cities we read about Paul traveling through in Acts, as well as letters to two pastors (Timothy and Titus), and one Christian friend (Philemon).

Paul wrote his letter to the Romans, probably during his third missionary journey while in the city of Corinth. The first half of Romans (chapters 1–8) presents the most thorough explanation of the doctrine of salvation found in the entire New Testament. Chapters 1–3 demonstrate mankind's guilt over sin and man's inability to save himself. Only when we understand ourselves as hopelessly lost and condemned sinners can we appreciate and respond to God's saving grace presented in the following chapters.

APPLICATION

In order for a person to have a relationship with God, he must understand his guilty condition and turn to Christ, the only means of rescue from God's wrath. If you're convinced you're not guilty, why would you need a Saviour? So Paul sets out to make perfectly clear, in his letter to the Romans, how our sin has separated us from God.

Paul describes a dark, downward regression, with men turning their backs on God, worshiping and serving the creature more than the Creator (1:25). What an effective description of idolatry, selfishness, and materialism! Paul describes several categories of sin, some more gruesome than others, but throughout his examples we see ourselves—and we know that we are a part of this broken, rebellious race of people. We are "without excuse" (1:20, 2:1).

Then Paul takes aim at the religious people—the ones who think their t-crossing and i-dotting and rule-keeping will impress God. The most diligently religious among us are *still* guilty, in need of a Saviour. To the Jews living in Rome, Paul explains, keeping "the law"—the moral and religious codes given by Moses—doesn't erase their sin.

No one ever completely obeyed *all* the rules for their *entire* lives, so instead of being a means to righteousness, the law merely reveals sin: "by the law is the knowledge of sin" (3:20). The law is so impossible to keep that it renders "every mouth…stopped [shut], and all the world…guilty before God" (3:19). But Paul will go on to describe how we can become "justified by faith without the deeds of the law" (3:28).

Why is this passage important if you have already received Christ? Because we often forget how tragically lost we would be without Him. Being reminded of this creates a sense of humility in our hearts, gratitude toward the Lord, and urgency in sharing the good news of God's grace with those who still need Him.

Father, I'm so thankful that You devised a means by which I could be forgiven and brought into a relationship with You for eternity, which isn't based on my good works. I could never have been *good enough* to earn Heaven. Thank You for not sending our entire race careening into Hell, but instead sending Your Son as the solution to our sin problem. How could I ever thank You enough?

"Being justified freely by his grace through the redemption that is in Christ Jesus:"

Romans 3:24

DAY 40

ROMANS 4–6

Our Faith Like Abraham's, Our Failure with Adam, and Our New Life in Christ

OVERVIEW

Chapter 4 continues to illustrate that salvation is not earned by works, but rather is received by faith, using Abraham's example. When we believe God as he did, God's righteousness is applied to our account, just as it was to his. Chapter 5 reveals the significance of Christ's death on the cross by contrasting Him with Adam. In Adam, our common forefather, everyone falls into sin that leads to *death*, but those who come to Christ are raised to *life*. Chapter 6 answers a logical question: if salvation is by grace, then should I just go ahead and sin willfully? Paul explains that just as Christ died on the cross and was raised back to life, a believer's old life has died and he too has been "raised…to walk in newness of life" (6:4).

APPLICATION

As Christians, we celebrate that we have been made free. Jesus Himself said, "If the Son therefore shall make you free, ye shall be free indeed" (John 8:36). But what does freedom mean?

Some believers have an incorrect definition of freedom that, to them, means doing whatever they want, when they want, and how they want—even if it's something that violates clear, biblical principles. And if some loving mentor attempts to challenge them, they cry out, "I'm free in Christ." But is that really what Christ intended?

Suppose a kind and loving man rescues a sweet young woman from an abusive environment, and they fall in love and marry. Has she been made free? Yes! She's been made free from her dreadful situation. But does that mean she's free to date other men? Is she free to commit adultery (2 Corinthians 11:2)?

We are not free in the *free-to-do-whatever* sense of the word. We have been freed from a cruel master (sin) to be made the servant of a wonderful new Master, Jesus. "But now being made free from sin, and become servants to God" (6:22).

Being free means we no longer belong to evil's side and we are under no obligation to do what our sinful temptations demand we do. And while freedom does include liberty (as in, I'm liberated from the toil of appeasing God for my guilt), it doesn't include a license to sin. God forbid (6:2, 6:15).

Freedom in Christ is so much better than "freedom" to live in the bondage of our sinful desires. It is instead the freedom to break free from sinful actions and habits, and, liberated by the grace of God, to live according to our new nature in Christ.

Father, thank You for freeing me from the dominion of sin by Your grace and through the sacrifice of Your Son! Thank You that I don't have to sin any longer. Sin's power in my life was put to death on the cross with Christ. And the same power that raised Jesus from the grave has raised me to walk in newness of life. May I live up to that great privilege today. May I refuse my flesh's tendency to do what sin wants it to do, reminding myself that I'm under no obligation to do so.

"Being then made free from sin, ye became the servants of righteousness."

Romans 6:18

DAY 41

ROMANS 7–8

Unable to Keep the Law, We Rest in God's Enduring Love

OVERVIEW

In today's Scripture passage, *the law* refers to the Old Testament commands for worship and daily living, given by God through Moses to the Jewish people. Believers in the first century struggled to understand the role of the law in their lives and whether they had an obligation to follow it. Furthermore, Jews who rejected Christ and His substitutionary atonement saw keeping the law as their means for salvation. So Paul explains that the law is not God's end-game. Grace is. The law can't save. It offers no life. It's impossible to fully keep. Instead of stressing over whether you have kept the law, God's plan is for you to live a Spirit-directed life, Paul explains. His Spirit will produce a spiritual vitality within us that the law never could. And God's love and grace provides us acceptance with Him that keeping the law never could.

APPLICATION

Can you identify with Paul when he says the things (sin) he doesn't want to do, he finds himself doing, and the things he does want to do (righteous acts), he finds himself unable to do (7:15–21)? I certainly identify with that. This cycle of good intentions turned to failed intentions that occurs in our lives is a giant source of discouragement for many believers. That's why we need Romans 7 and 8.

Romans 7 tells us this is normal. That doesn't mean it's right. But it happens to the best of us. It happened in Paul's life; it happens in my life; and I know it happens in your life. Paul helps us by separating the behavior from the believer. "It is no more I that do it, but sin that dwelleth in me (my flesh)" (7:17). It's not you. It's sin. It's your flesh. Every believer walking on earth has it. And it—the flesh—is why we still sin. We still need to confess it and forsake it and learn to overcome it. But we shouldn't be surprised by it. And it shouldn't shake our faith. Confess it, accept God's forgiveness, and then be grateful for His grace.

Romans 8 tells us how God sees the situation. And this is really important. This reality—the presence of flesh and therefore sin—does not cause God to expel you. He hasn't given up on you, He doesn't condemn you (8:1), He hasn't stopped loving you. Stop thinking there must be something wrong with you. Stop thinking, "I can't do it" just because you have failed a few hundred times. God does *not* condemn you. Not because He's blind (He's not) and not because you're good (you're not), but because of *Christ*. The righteous merit of Jesus has been gifted to you. God is "for you" (8:31), and *nothing*—can separate you from His love (8:38–39).

This truth doesn't minimize sin. It elevates and celebrates grace. So if you have accepted Christ, then step forward into this day knowing that you're flawed but forgiven. And expect, today, that God intends to guide, favor, and use you. And if you haven't yet accepted Christ, do it now!

Father, thank You for Your enduring, unshakable, unconditional love! I praise You for the depth and length of Your grace, which makes me accepted and forgiven. I thank You that You don't condemn me and that You've promised not to. And all of this is because of the merit and sacrifice of your Son. Thank You, Lord.

"For I am persuaded, that neither death, nor life, nor angels, nor principalities, nor powers, nor things present, nor things to come, nor height, nor depth, nor any other creature, shall be able to separate us from the love of God, which is in Christ Jesus our Lord."

Romans 8:38–39

DAY 42

ROMANS 9–11

Paul's Heart for Israel; God's Heart for All People

OVERVIEW

Today's reading is a unique three-chapter segment within Romans because it addresses mostly the nation of Israel, who historically were God's special people (of whom Paul was a member). Paul sought to help the Jewish people understand a few things. First, he wanted them to know that it was God's (and his) desire for Jewish people to be saved by faith in Jesus Christ, their long-prophesied Messiah (9:3, 10:1). He also told them to know that they were not the only nation God was interested in. The Messiah's salvation was for all people from every nation. Anyone may come to God, if they come through Christ.

APPLICATION

God's sovereignty is described throughout today's passage, including 9:10–24 where Esau and Pharaoh are used as illustrations. For centuries, Bible students have debated their understanding of the balance between these two truths:

- God's sovereignty: He is in charge of all things.
- Mankind's responsibility: We must make a decision to believe on Christ.

For me, the illustration of Pharaoh helps: God creates people (like Pharaoh) even though He foreknows they will reject and oppose Him, because He is capable of sovereignly governing their lives to fulfill His purposes. It is simultaneously true that Pharaoh was responsible for his rejection of God *and* that God was sovereign in His design of how Pharaoh's disobedience and rebellion would be used for His eternal purposes. These two parallel truths still apply to unbelievers today.

This is encouraging. Our Sovereign God isn't waiting for history to unfold and then coming up with alternative plans based on what mankind throws His way.

God inhabits eternity. He rules the universe. He knows all things—past, present, and future.

This does not mean, however, that mankind should throw his hands up and relinquish God's call to make decisions and make a difference. "Make a difference?" you wonder? How can we—who are not sovereign—possibly make a difference? We make a difference by submitting to and cooperating with God's leadership in our lives. As we do, He perfectly fits our imperfect efforts into His perfect plan. You see, God used Pharaoh, against Pharaoh's will. But God can use us as willing agents in cooperation with Him. What a privilege and opportunity!

Another important application from these chapters is that mankind's responsibility to believe on Christ is woven throughout this passage, as is the believers' responsibility to share Christ with the world (10:13–14). This eliminates the notion that God's sovereignty excuses us from evangelism and fervent service in the cause of Christ. (See in particular 9:30–32, 10:3, 10:9, 11:20–23, 11:30–32.)

Finally, it's okay if we don't fully understand this topic, this side of eternity (11:33–35). It won't be the only thing about God's ways that is beyond our understanding (Isaiah 55:8–9).

Lord God, I'm thankful that I know the Creator of and Sovereign Lord over all things. I'm thankful to be Your child, Your servant, Your friend. And I'm so thankful for the assurance of knowing You work all things together for my good as You sovereignly fulfill Your purposes. I trust You as You unfold Your plan in and around my life.

"For whosoever shall call upon the name of the Lord shall be saved."

Romans 10:13

DAY 43

ROMANS 12–13

Paul's Counsel for Dealing with Spiritual Siblings and Civic Authorities

OVERVIEW

In chapter 12, Romans shifts from theological instruction to practical application. It starts with, "I beseech you therefore, brethren, by the mercies of God." Based on the first eleven chapters' discussion of God's great mercy toward undeserving mankind, it's our "reasonable service" (12:1) to present our lives to Him as an offering. After discussing our surrender to God (12:1–2), Paul goes on to give exhortations concerning our service to the church body (12:4–8), our spirit toward fellow believers (12:9–21), our submission to government (13:1–7), and our spiritual walk (13:8–14).

APPLICATION

Relationships are life's building blocks. Your quality of life, in many ways, hinges on the quality of your relationships. The most important thing in life is establishing a relationship with God. Most other significant things in life revolve around our human relationships.

So, the instructions on relationships found in 12:9–21 are vital for us to master. In these thirteen verses, there are thirty-one little staccato-style directives (twenty-three "dos" and eight "don'ts"). These instructions focus on our inner character, our outer behaviors, and our responses when wronged.

Relationships begin with *character*. We are to possess charity (vv. 9–10), purity (v. 9), dependability (v. 11), and resilience (v. 12). Think about how critically important those four traits are to healthy marriages and families or relationships in the church. Your character is shaping your relationships—for good or bad.

Relationships require right *behaviors*. We must learn to behave generously (v. 13), practice hospitality (v. 13), show empathy (v. 15), and live with humility (v. 16). These actions deepen, strengthen, and nurture our relationships.

Relationships are tested when we are wronged. When people fail us, how will we *respond*? Author Emerson Eggerichs says it this way: "My response is my responsibility." Vulnerability is needed (vv. 14, 17, 19–20). Honesty is critical (v. 17). And civility is necessary (v. 18). If we respond in these ways, we can, as verse 21 says, "overcome evil with good."

How's your character? How's your behavior? How's your response? The sum of those things, over time, equals the quality of your relationships. I hope you'll follow God's counsel, given through Paul, in one or more of your relationships today.

Lord, thank You for Your great mercies! I recognize that it's my "reasonable service" to offer my life to You. You're worthy of that—and so much more! Help me relate to my fellow believers and others in the ways You have instructed me. Thank You for providing me, in Your Word, not only profound eternal truths, but also simple, practical advice for daily living. May I follow Your ways every day!

"Be kindly affectioned one to another with brotherly love;
in honour preferring one another;"

Romans 12:10

DAY 44

ROMANS 14–16

Paul's Final Greetings, Salutations, and Exhortations

OVERVIEW

The closing chapters of Romans are more personal in nature, as Paul speaks to the Roman believers about his desire to visit them, shares about his current journeys, and mentions specific believers in Rome who he asks to be greeted on his behalf (chapters 15–16). But before he gets to these final greetings, Paul needs to exhort the Roman believers on how to manage disagreements over matters of preference among fellow believers (chapter 14).

APPLICATION

As believers, we have the responsibility of applying God's Word to the daily detail of our lives, with as much specificity as possible. This is a healthy part of the sanctification process—obeying and implementing God's timeless commands and principles in our own day and time.

Because of our varying backgrounds, perspectives, experiences, personalities, circumstances, and surrounding cultures, it's not surprising that some believers end up applying biblical principles differently from others. There's room for this variation in preferences within the family of God. But Paul knew that these differences, if not understood and respected by one another, would threaten to cause division among otherwise like-minded people.

There are several areas where the Bible is crystal clear (honesty, integrity, moral purity, etc.). But what about areas where there is room for interpretation or a spectrum of how a particular principle is applied? How do we deal with the inevitable conflict when how we see something differs from how another brother or sister in Christ sees it? Romans 14 provides three guidelines for handling this dilemma:

- Don't let your difference create conflict with your brother in Christ (v. 3). Instead, respect his right to come to his own sincere conclusion (v. 5).
- Don't set yourself up as your brother's judge (v. 10). Instead, remember that we will each give a personal account to Jesus Christ (v. 12). Only then will we all know where we got it right and where we missed the mark.
- Don't focus your energy on your differences or insist on your way (vv. 15, 21). Instead, focus on the areas where you can agree, encourage, and strengthen each other (v. 19).

If we'll practice these guidelines, we will enjoy the liberty of knowing some of our brothers and sisters apply the Word in their lives a bit differently from the way we do and still be able to love and appreciate them while serving the Lord together with fervency and unity.

Father, help me resist the temptation to set myself up as the judge and jury in other people's lives. Help me focus on my own accountability to You and seek to be thoroughly right with You in humility and in truth. Give me Spirit-directed wisdom to bring the details of my life in line with Your Word. And then enable me to trust You to do the same for others, without my oversight. And may I prepare today for the day when I will stand before You personally.

"Let us therefore follow after the things which make for peace, and things wherewith one may edify another."

Romans 14:19

DAY 45

1 CORINTHIANS 1–4

Correcting Division and Asserting God's Wisdom

OVERVIEW

Corinth is located in Greece, approximately fifty miles west of Athens. The church there, to whom this letter was written, was founded during Paul's second missionary journey. We read about it ten days ago in Acts 18. Paul writes this letter a few years later to correct several behavioral and belief problems reported to exist among the congregation.

The first four chapters deal with the problem of division. The church was developing cliques and factions based on people's personality preferences. Some members were fans of Apollos (a godly and gifted teacher), others thought more highly of Paul, while others preferred Peter (called Cephas here). What's ironic is that none of these men would have wanted a following of splintered members. What they all wanted—and what the Lord wanted—was for the church to function in unity and harmony.

APPLICATION

Paul knew that if the division occurring in the Corinthian church continued, it would threaten the church's very existence. This division stemmed from immaturity and a lingering carnality which the believers needed to outgrow (*carnal* in 3:3—behaving in a fleshly rather than a spiritual manner). A loving but firm confrontation was in order.

In God's economy, leaders don't contend for popularity, position, or prominence like the world's leaders do. (1:18–2:16 contrasts the world's wisdom with God's.) God's leaders aren't concerned about who gets the credit or who gets assigned which responsibility, because their goal is to advance the name and kingdom of Christ, not their own names or empires.

God's leaders are mere servants (3:5) who fulfill different roles within God's work. They're not in competition with one another—their efforts work in tandem (3:6). They don't take credit, because they know they aren't the ones who make the fruit grow—only God can do that!

Christian servants must never view one another as competitors but as members of the same team. "Now he that planteth and he that watereth are one" (3:8a). And they must remember, our faithful God is watching over their service, "and every man shall receive his own reward according to his own labor" (3:8b).

We can rejoice to know—if we stay unified—that not only does our Father permit us the great honor of being "laborers together with God" (3:9), but He also rewards us for the very service He enables.

There are many sources for potential division in a church. They are most often issues of preference or personality, which are given far greater attention than they deserve. God's counsel to us is "that there be no divisions among you; but that ye be perfectly joined together in the same mind" (1:10) and "that no one of you be puffed up for one against another" (4:6).

Father, thank You for enlisting me in Your service and for the privilege of being a laborer with You. Thank You for enabling me for the work You have called me to do. Please help me be a unifying influence in my church and among other believers, never a dividing influence. May the service I render be *for You* and *with You*.

"For we are labourers together with God: ye are God's husbandry, ye are God's building."

1 Corinthians 3:9

DAY 46

1 CORINTHIANS 5–7

Confronting Immorality in the Church

OVERVIEW

As Paul continues to address the various problems plaguing the Corinthian congregation, he shifts his focus to sexual sin. The Bible teaches that marital intimacy is the good, joyous, and healthy invention of God. But as with other good things, it can become a sinful idol when used outside God's boundaries. Corinthian church members were engaging in related ungodly behavior and needed to be confronted.

God's simple and profoundly wise design is that this gift of God be enjoyed between one man and one woman in the covenant of marriage. Any deviation from that standard, according to the Bible, is sin and is referred to broadly as "fornication."

APPLICATION

Our culture's values and beliefs concerning human sexuality have gone off the rails. And the condition of our society, our families, and our churches are not better for it. Almost overnight, in the last half generation, mankind's departure from God's moral standards has accelerated in a rapid departure from God's design.

Let's not be naive. We have *always* lived in a sexually-broken culture. History is filled with scandalous stories of immorality. So *that* is not new. But today's normalization of fornication along with the troubling deviations from God's design (such as same-sex relationships and gender confusion) demand with greater urgency that believers take their stand and embrace the purity taught in the New Testament.

- We must guard our *hearts* against impurity by safeguarding what we see, hear, and are influenced by (Proverbs 4:23).
- We must guard our *minds* against adopting culture's sexual idolatry and redefining of values; we must constantly tie our thinking to Scripture instead of culture.

- We must guard our *children* by teaching the truth, opening up dialogue, and protecting them from an out-of-control, sex-crazed entertainment industry.
- We must guard our *marriages* against the tragedy of adultery by cultivating healthy relationships and setting up boundaries to protect from temptation.
- We must guard our *churches* by not neglecting our responsibility to confront sin and, by our neglect, condoning it.

We who are members of the body of Christ must provide a clear contrast of purity (Ephesians 5:27) to our broken and confused world, demonstrating the joy and blessedness of biblical morality along with happy, healthy marriages. As they see these realities in us, some who have been wounded by sin will, by the brightness of our witness, come to Christ for cleansing, healing, and restoration.

Father, please protect me from sin. Lead me not into temptation, but deliver me from evil. I confess that I'm sometimes tempted by the flesh within me, the world around me, and the devil beneath me. Please not only protect me, but also use me as an encouragement to others concerning the value of a pure life. Especially, Lord, use me and my generation to help provide a holy example for the next generation.

"What? know ye not that your body is the temple of the Holy Ghost which is in you, which ye have of God, and ye are not your own? For ye are bought with a price: therefore glorify God in your body, and in your spirit, which are God's."

1 Corinthians 6:19–20

DAY 47

1 CORINTHIANS 8–11

Practical Principles for Daily Choices in Christian Living

OVERVIEW

In today's portion of this epistle, Paul guides the Corinthian Christians on the question of whether to eat meat that had been sacrificed to pagan idols (chapters 8 and 10). He provides perspective on the role of church leadership, including how the churches are obligated to support those who preach the Word (chapter 9). And he corrects their misuse of the Lord's Table (chapter 11). This ordinance is not a time to indulge our appetites but rather to reflect on Christ and examine our individual lives.

APPLICATION

Believers in the first century had a question that we don't face in twenty-first century America: Is it wrong to eat meat that has been sacrificed to idols? After pagan worshipers sacrificed animals to false deities, they salvaged the usable cuts of meat to sell in the local market. Would partaking of that meat violate the Christian's belief that "to us there is but one God" (8:6)?

Paul's answer? No…and yes. No, it's not going to injure our spiritual health. We're neither "better" nor "worse" (8:8). We have liberty to eat it. All meat ultimately belongs to God (10:26, 28). But there were larger questions Paul wanted *mature* believers to ask. Paul's conviction was that though we are *free* to eat meat sacrificed to idols, we *shouldn't*, because "this liberty of yours [would] become a stumblingblock to them that are weak" (8:9).

Why should this matter to you and me since this issue doesn't come into play at our local grocery store or steak house? It matters because, while we don't face the same specific issue, we do face the same principle.

Some Christians seem to live their lives on the far edge of the gray area that exists between *clearly right* and *clearly wrong*. The question immature Christians use in their rationalization is: *What's wrong with ______?* Paul's letter expresses that maybe that's not the best approach. According to Paul, the questions we ought to be asking are these:

- Does this choice hinder my ability to advance the gospel (9:12)?
- Does this choice build up (edify) other believers (10:23)?
- Does this choice bring glory to God (10:31)?

Are we willing to limit our liberty in order to provide the clearest witness and set the best example? While this doesn't authorize us to police the lives of others as self-appointed judges, it does provide us with a helpful matrix in making our own choices.

As you face the endless opportunities that today's culture sets before you, consider using Paul's criteria to make the *best* choices, not just the technically-acceptable ones.

Father, thank You for the liberty I have in You and for the grace that You extend to me because of the cross. I'm truly thankful that I don't have to obsess over some complicated system to keep You satisfied or panic over whether I have met Your expectations. In this freedom, however, I do want to ask for wisdom. I want to do what most glorifies You, strengthens others, and provides the best witness. Please guide me today that these outcomes might be the reality of my life.

"Whether therefore ye eat, or drink, or whatsoever ye do, do all to the glory of God."

1 Corinthians 10:31

DAY 48

1 CORINTHIANS 12–14

A Body That Functions, Love That Endures, and Worship That Is Orderly

OVERVIEW

Paul continues to help the church members in Corinth learn what it means to function as God intended. Today's three chapters divide into three clear themes. Chapter 12 discusses how the local church, composed of individual and unique members, is to work together in harmony. Chapter 13 describes what godly love looks like in relationships. And chapter 14 addresses their need to bring order to their chaotic and confusing worship gatherings.

APPLICATION

The institution of the local church is truly a beautiful thing! It was God's idea, and when it functions according to His design, there's no limit to the impact it can make by His grace.

The "body" was Paul's favorite metaphor for the church (Romans 12:4–5, Ephesians 1:23, 4:12, Colossians 1:24, 2:19, and here in 1 Corinthians 12). Just as our human bodies are made up of individual and unique parts—eyes, ears, nose, head, hands, feet—so the church is composed of individual and unique "members." Like our bodies, the church is only able to accomplish its mission if the members are functioning. . .and functioning in harmony.

The metaphor of the body reveals the value of:

- Unity—we are designed to function as one (12:12, 20, 25).
- Purpose—we have each been added according to God's wise design (12:18).
- Uniqueness—we are each intended to contribute something unique (12:15–19).
- Interdependence—we need each other in order to fully function (12:21, 25–26).

So instead of comparing ourselves with others (12:15–16), creating division (12:25), or sitting on the sidelines, we must each get plugged in. We must find our place to contribute and faithfully carry out our own roles in the body, appreciating and flexing with one another along the way.

Christ loves the church (Ephesians 5:25), and He has chosen the local church as the vehicle to carry the gospel message to the "uttermost part of the earth" (Acts 1:8). These facts give great significance to the church and our responsibility to contribute to its health. Let's make a difference in and through our churches by being fully engaged and functioning members of that beautiful, local body of Christ.

Lord Jesus, thank You for placing me in Your body, the church. It's a privilege to be joined to You. I recognize that You knew what You were doing when You led me to my current local assembly, and there's a job You have for me to fulfill. Please empower and enable me to do it! Also, help me cultivate unity and mutual appreciation among my fellow members. Thank You for them, too, Lord! May You receive great glory through our service to You.

"For as the body is one, and hath many members, and all the members of that one body, being many, are one body: so also is Christ."

1 Corinthians 12:12

DAY 49

1 CORINTHIANS 15–16

The Importance and Implications of Christ's Resurrection and the Conclusion of This Letter

OVERVIEW

The final issue Paul confronts in Corinth is the most important: the resurrection of Jesus Christ. A group of false teachers was questioning the resurrection—both Christ's historical resurrection and the believers' eventual resurrection. They said such a concept was impossible and that life simply ends in death. To strengthen the believers' faith, Paul begins by defining "the gospel" as the death, burial, *and resurrection* of Jesus (15:1–4). He goes on to explain that Christ's resurrection makes our future resurrection possible. In the final chapter, Paul forecasts his travel itinerary and shares greetings from mutual friends of the Corinthian Christians.

APPLICATION

According to Paul (who wrote under God's supernatural guidance), Christ's resurrection is the truth on which our entire faith and future depends. If Christ didn't rise from the grave, our faith is useless (v. 17). Our efforts in evangelism are wasted (v. 14). Our sins are still stacked against us (v. 17). There's no life after death, because we won't rise either (v. 18). If He didn't rise, there's no reason for joy, because this broken, earthly life is all there is (v. 19). But He *did* rise from the grave (v. 20), so we have hope, purpose, and joy. Death is not final, and eternity with our Saviour awaits us!

Did you know there are actually religious denominations and clergy that consider themselves Christian but question or deny that Christ's resurrection was literal, as the Bible describes it? It's no surprise that attendance in these churches has diminished to the point that many have closed their doors. If Christ didn't rise, why even bother?

The truth of the resurrection changes everything about the end of our story. But it should also influence our daily lives, here and now, in the middle of our story. How? Check out the final verse of chapter 15, the longest of all Paul's chapters (v. 58). Paul says, because of the resurrection, we should be "stedfast, unmoveable, always abounding in the work of the Lord, forasmuch as ye know that your labour is not in vain in the Lord."

Allow me to rephrase: Be faithful! Don't give up! Keep serving! Go above and beyond in your service to Christ and in your efforts to reach others! Because of the resurrection, your faithfulness matters not only for time, but for all eternity.

What an encouragement. What a motivating truth to live for Christ today!

Lord Jesus, I praise You for Your resurrection power. I praise You for the fact that death could not defeat You and the grave could not hold You! Thank You for sharing Your victory with me. Without You I'd be hopeless and condemned to suffer forever in punishment earned by my sin. But because of You, I have hope and eternal life. Thank You. May I serve You with joy, fervor, and eternity in view today.

"Therefore, my beloved brethren, be ye stedfast, unmoveable, always abounding in the work of the Lord, forasmuch as ye know that your labour is not in vain in the Lord."

1 Corinthians 15:58

DAY 50

2 CORINTHIANS 1–3

Paul Reviews His Relationship with the Corinthians

OVERVIEW

Paul's second letter to the Christians in Corinth takes on a more personal tone than the first and doesn't focus as much on confronting error. Apparently, the believers responded positively to the first letter, correcting the errors of their ways. The opening chapters include Paul's perspective on suffering and difficulty. He also speaks specifically about his and his colleagues' ministry among the Corinthians, including the confrontation of the first letter. He acknowledges the influence he has had among the Corinthians with humility, gratitude, and grace.

APPLICATION

What is it that you have been called of God to do? Are you married? A parent? Do you have the responsibility of teaching the Bible in your church? Is there someone to whom God wants you to witness? Do you have a job? Is there a task for the glory and purposes of God that you hope to accomplish?

When you get right down to it, all of these roles and responsibilities are over our heads. If we're honest, we know we're not up to it. Others may not be aware of our inadequacies in the areas listed above, but we sure are. We know how often we fail to meet our own expectations. We know how often our behavior doesn't meet our intentions.

What should we do about this problem? Should we resign? Give up? Walk away from any responsibility that affects others because we know we'll let them down? I don't think so.

Here's the reality: the only people available to do any and all of the jobs God has for people to do, here and now, are imperfect people. So don't bail out! Here's a better idea: seek God's enabling.

An experienced Christian once said to me, "You know that gap between your capability and what needs to be done? That's where God operates. And because He does, He receives the glory." I think she had it right. And I think of her words when I read 2 Corinthians 3:5–6.

Paul didn't serve God because he was sufficient to the task. Paul served God because *God* was sufficient to the task! Here's the good news: God delights in making you sufficient for what He's called you to accomplish. Because when He enables you, not only are His purposes advanced, but His glory is elevated. And you and I experience the thrill of being part of God at work—in us, around us, and through us. What a privilege!

Lord, thank You for not only calling me to serve You, but also for enabling me. I confess and acknowledge my insufficiency when it comes to the work You have called me to do. Keep me humble, but use me far beyond my capability to accomplish all that You will. I ask this with Your pleasure and glory in mind.

"Not that we are sufficient of ourselves to think any thing as of ourselves; but our sufficiency is of God; Who also hath made us able ministers of the new testament...."

2 Corinthians 3:5–6

DAY 51

2 CORINTHIANS 4–6

Paul's Approach to Gospel Ministry

OVERVIEW

Today's passage is biographical in nature—a memoir of sorts of Paul's ministry legacy. He describes his motivation for ministry, Christ's enabling him for ministry, his attitude toward difficulty in ministry, and his heart for the people he served and led.

APPLICATION

Paul shares his perspective on what it means to serve the Lord as a gospel-preaching, church-planting missionary. But the spirit of what he shares really applies to all New Testament believers. Paul is an example to all of us, not just those who serve in vocational ministry. Consider the terminology Paul used to describe himself and those who served with him:

- "Ourselves your servants for Jesus' sake" (4:5). We should learn to view ourselves merely as servants in the work of the Lord, serving Him and serving people, as unto Him.
- "We are ambassadors for Christ" (5:20). We are the Lord's representatives on this earth—carrying His name. We must acknowledge this role, accept the responsibilities of keeping our testimony bright, and faithfully share the gospel with others.
- "We then, as workers together with him" (6:1). Be encouraged—we don't serve alone! We are working with others and, most importantly, with the Lord. We don't invite God to join *us* in *our activity*. It is He who invited us to become involved in *His*.

To serve God is man's greatest privilege. Not everyone is called to full-time, vocational ministry, but every Christian is a full-time minister of the gospel. Paul likens the gospel minister to an "earthen vessel" (4:7). Despite being weak, imperfect, and common, we can be used by God when we present ourselves as empty channels for His service. God uses fragile, ordinary instruments to demonstrate the power of the gospel, making it unmistakable that the source of all spiritual power is God Himself. And because of that, He receives all the glory. Our *ordinariness* becomes the very vehicle for God's *extraordinariness*.

Lord, thank You for making me Your child, Your servant, and Your ambassador. What a privilege! Please enable me with the power that comes only from You to serve You fruitfully and faithfully. Keep my eyes focused on You, serving You for the right reasons—to increase Your glory, bring You pleasure, and advance Your purposes.

"But we have this treasure in earthen vessels, that the excellency of the power may be of God, and not of us."

2 Corinthians 4:7

DAY 52

2 CORINTHIANS 7–9

A Commendation for Repentance and an Exhortation on Generosity

OVERVIEW

In chapter 7 Paul expresses his gratitude over the Corinthians' response to his first letter. He did not enjoy making them feel sorry. But he was glad that by making them sorry they repented and put their errors behind them.

Then, in chapters 8–9, Paul challenges the believers in Corinth to be generous. Paul was planning to receive an offering from the more financially stable churches in Europe, where Corinth was, to meet the needs in Jerusalem where saints were struggling to meet their basic needs. Apparently, he had discussed this with the church at Corinth a year prior and they had committed to give, but their actions had not yet caught up with their promises. Paul used the example of the Macedonian Christians to challenge and inspire the Corinthian Christians in this offering.

APPLICATION

When it came to challenging believers to give to the work of God, Paul didn't employ gimmicky methods (no raffles or bingo tournaments) or manipulative techniques. Paul spoke directly to their hearts, appealing to their spiritual senses.

He challenged them to be generous and eager to give (8:4). Financial contributions to the Lord's work are not a "necessary evil" or obligation. They are offerings of gratitude (9:15), motivated by a divine work of grace in the heart of the giver (8:6–7).

When we give offerings to the Lord, through His church, we do so with Jesus Himself in mind, never losing sight of the extraordinary sacrifice He made for us. "For ye know the grace of our Lord Jesus Christ, that, though he was rich, yet for your sakes he became poor, that ye through his poverty might be rich" (8:9).

As we mature in our faith, as the Corinthians did, we learn to give willingly (8:12), proportionately (8:13–15), expectantly (9:6), and even cheerfully (9:7).

And, best of all, when we give faithfully and sacrificially to the Lord, we are able to confidently rest in His promises to meet each of our needs (8:12–15). We won't do without for having given to the Lord. That's the part that's so miraculous! And that's the part that requires faith.

In Paul's agricultural analogy, which likened financial giving to planting (sowing) seeds, he said that God would both provide the planter with the seeds to plant, while at the same time providing that same planter with plenty of seeds for his own household's bread (9:10–11). So many faithful servants of God have observed, "You simply can't outgive God."

And you can take that to the bank.

Lord, when I get caught in the flow of today's materialistic consumer culture, I sometimes forget how truly generous You have been to me. Thank You (I don't say that enough). If You never give me another thing, thank You for all that You have already given. And thank You, mostly, for the gift of Your Son—the most unspeakable gift of all time. Guide me and provide for me in my giving back to You, Lord. And, as You do, please receive my gifts as an offering of love and gratitude. You are worthy.

"Every man according as he purposeth in his heart, so let him give; not grudgingly, or of necessity: for God loveth a cheerful giver."

2 Corinthians 9:7

DAY 53

2 CORINTHIANS 10–13

Paul Defends His Spiritual Authority

OVERVIEW

Apparently, there were competitive forces at work in Corinth, undermining the Apostle Paul's influence in people's lives. Some were outright heretical teachers, while others may have simply cast doubt in the hearts of the believers through a slow and steady campaign of questioning. Paul spends nearly all of these four chapters defending himself (sad, isn't it, after all he'd done for the Corinthians?), reiterating his spiritual credential, and expressing his heart of genuine love for the believers.

APPLICATION

One of the most personal sections amidst all of Paul's epistles appears in 12:7–10, when he describes his "thorn in the flesh." This was a case of unanswered prayer for the apostle: "I besought the Lord thrice, that it might depart from me" (v. 8). The "thorn" was apparently a physical malady that caused pain, irritation, and difficulty. Some have speculated that it may have been a disease related to the apostle's eyes, based on Galatians 4:15.

Satan used this difficulty as a means of attack, in spite of Paul's giant-like faith (v. 7). We should assume Satan will attack us, too, with difficulty and discouragement.

God's response to Paul's prayer was—instead of giving him deliverance from the pain—that He would give him a special measure of His grace, strength, and power. A careful reading of Paul's testimony will reveal three powerful truths:

- The one thing Paul wanted more than comfort was the power and presence of Christ in his life. "Most gladly therefore will I rather glory in my infirmities, that the power of Christ may rest upon me" (v. 9). How badly do you long to be filled with God's presence?
- God often chooses to infuse us with power and usefulness, specifically through the means of pain. God doesn't cause the pain, but He repurposes

what Satan intends to use for evil, using it instead for good. This is why Paul could take pleasure in infirmities (v. 9).

- God isn't looking for strong people to use. In fact, He's uniquely interested in pouring out His strength on the weak—those who have nothing to offer. "When I am weak, then am I strong" (v. 10). In this, He receives greater glory and enjoys lavishing His grace on and through His children.

Do you have a thorn in the flesh? Let God use it for your good today!

Lord, thank You for being willing to share Your grace, strength, and power with a weak one such as me. I trust You with the pains of life. If they allow me to be more fully used of You, or if they allow me to experience greater depth in my relationship with You, then I accept them as benefits. Thank You for Your grace, made available to me by the death and resurrection of Your Son, Jesus.

"And he said unto me, My grace is sufficient for thee: for my strength is made perfect in weakness. Most gladly therefore will I rather glory in my infirmities, that the power of Christ may rest upon me."

2 Corinthians 12:9

DAY 54

GALATIANS 1–2

There Is No Other Gospel

OVERVIEW

All of Paul's other letters to churches are addressed to believers in one particular city. But this letter is written to several churches in a region: the Roman province of Galatia. So this letter would have been circulated among the churches in four Galatian cities, which Paul founded during his first missionary journey: Antioch (the one in Pisidia, not Syria), Iconium, Lystra, and Derbe.

A false teaching had begun to work its way into these churches, and Paul urgently and firmly confronted the issue. The message was that Gentiles wishing to become Christians needed to convert to Judaism and follow the law of Moses to be truly saved. This message directly contradicted the true gospel, that salvation is by grace through faith alone.

APPLICATION

If anyone was going to attempt to use their Jewish religious credentials to earn a place in Heaven, it could have been Paul. He had been trained by the greatest Jewish scholars, had kept all the rules, and had been an up-and-coming power player within the elite sect of Pharisee rabbis. But he came to realize the emptiness of all that when Christ saved his soul.

There's a tendency in all of us to assume that our acceptance with God is tied to our earthly performance. Our proud, independent human nature seeks to be "good enough" to earn our ticket to Heaven. False religions lay out varying road maps on how one arrives at his own redemption. But the two-edged message of Christ's gospel is this: He offers Heaven freely to all who come by faith to Him, but this saving grace is only for those willing to admit they're not good enough to earn their own way.

Paul laid all of his Jewish religious credentials down, never to be picked up again, because he knew they had gained him nothing of authentic spiritual value. He had placed his soul in the hands of Jesus Christ with the same utterly-dependent faith as the most irreligious heathen. All of his past bragging rights now meant nothing; they were crucified like Christ. Now his identity was wrapped up in one thing: Christ. Now his life was all about living for Christ, being indwelled by Christ, following Christ, rejoicing in Christ's love, and resting in Christ's sacrifice. That's the message of Galatians 2:20.

I hope this is your testimony too—not only that you have received Christ, but also that your daily life is wrapped up in and defined by Him. I hope you're not struggling to find acceptance or satisfaction through some stressful pursuit of good-enough behavior, but that you're rejoicing in the One who loves you in spite of you and laid down His life for you.

Lord Jesus, thank You for loving me. Thank You for giving Your life for me on the cross. I'm grateful that You live in me, that You live Your life through me. What an opportunity is mine—that You, the Creator and Redeemer, would live in and through me. May I be a yielded vessel, and may You receive the glory You're due through my crucified life.

"I am crucified with Christ: nevertheless I live; yet not I, but Christ liveth in me: and the life which I now live in the flesh I live by the faith of the Son of God, who loved me, and gave himself for me."

Galatians 2:20

DAY 55

GALATIANS 3–4

The Law Is Not a Means to Salvation but a Revealer that We Need Saving

OVERVIEW

Paul continues to address the key doctrine that is the theme of the entire letter: salvation by grace, through faith. Long before Moses gave the Jewish people the law, Abraham was promised an heir who would redeem mankind through faith (3:16). The law was given later to provide temporary guidance for faithful living (3:19) until the promise was fulfilled in God's perfect time, when Jesus Christ came as Messiah (4:1–5). The primary purpose of the law, since Christ has come, is to demonstrate how woefully short we all fall of God's holiness (3:22–24), revealing our need for a Saviour.

APPLICATION

The Christians in Galatia, most of whom were not Jewish, were beginning to wonder if they needed a crash course on Jewish customs and traditions to please their new Saviour, who came as a Jew and as the fulfillment of Jewish prophecy. They were fed this idea by legalistic "Judaizers" from Jerusalem who had infiltrated their ranks.

Paul's message in Galatians is, "Why turn back?" As a former strict, rule-keeping Jew himself, Paul well knew what a delight it was to experience the awesome liberty of grace where God provides acceptance through a vibrant relationship with Christ, instead of obligated adherence to complicated traditions.

Today, most of us who are believers were not saved out of Judaism. But we were saved out of *something*. And the message, "Don't go back!" applies to us too.

The Galatians must not turn back to the religious traditions that previously held them captive. But what held you captive? What was your life like before you received Christ? Or, what would your life be like, were it not for the grace of God? What sinful behaviors and destructive lifestyles would you be involved in? Our stories are different yet the same: we were enslaved to sin (Romans 6:17).

Paul's question (which is really God's question) to you in 4:9 is essentially, "Why would you ever want to go back to that tragic state of affairs, after having been set free by Christ?" And yet we do. We tamper with sin. We stray dangerously toward behaviors, attitudes, thoughts, and influences that are part of the old, sin-cursed life. And it doesn't make any sense.

Paul's question still stands. After all Christ has done for you, and after the wonderful deliverance and liberty He has provided for you, in time and eternity, why would you *even think* about going back?

Heavenly Father, thank You for setting me free from the bondage of sin. Thank You for adopting me as Your child. Thank You for not having me jump through hoops and satisfy complicated demands to be right with You. Thank You for making me, once and for all time, right with You through the cleansing blood of Your wonderful Son.

"But now, after that ye have known God, or rather are known of God, how turn ye again to the weak and beggarly elements, whereunto ye desire again to be in bondage?"

Galatians 4:9

DAY 56

GALATIANS 5–6

Following the Guidance of the Spirit Instead of the Flesh

OVERVIEW

In Paul's final argument against the Judaizers' attempt to bring the Galatians under the rule of the Old Testament law, he offers the ultimate alternative to the law—the Spirit of God. Instead of being bound by the law, Christians are to be led by the Spirit.

Circumcision is mentioned in today's passage and was used by Paul as a symbolic metaphor for one who is devoted to Jewish customs. Circumcision had long been considered the most distinctive identifier of a committed Jew. Paul was not making a case for or against the actual surgical procedure but was emphasizing that only Christ—not Judaism or any other religious pedigree—is of any value to our relationship with God.

APPLICATION

Some Galatians no doubt had a question as they got to this point in the letter, which went something like this: "If I'm free from the rules of the law, does that mean that I'm free to do whatever I want?" A God-engineered part of their conscience knew better than to conclude that.

No, indeed we are not free to do *whatever*. We are free to follow God. I have been freed from the bondage of both Moses' Law and the bondage of my sin. Both bondages are real, and I shouldn't trade one for another. That would be like jumping from the frying pan into the fire.

Then what's a Christian to do, Paul? And what's a Christian *not* to do?

It's simple (not easy). We are to deny the works of the flesh (most of which are obvious and can be identified with some precision by studying the epistles) and follow the moment-by-moment guidance of the Holy Spirit.

Sometimes we want to reduce the Christian life to a bullet-point list of dos and don'ts. But life's just not that simple. We could never list every scenario, and even if we could, we'd then be relying on the Judaizers' techniques and headed back toward legalistic bondage.

So God has given us the wonderful gift of the Holy Spirit. What a treasure! He is our companion, guide, teacher, and friend. He teaches us what is right and what is wrong, in real time. He illuminates the Word so we know how it applies to our situations. He convicts us when we have done wrong and then is quick to comfort us with the promise of forgiveness when we repent.

Check out 5:19–21 to discover the ugly, harsh, immoral behavior the flesh is capable of producing. Then check out 5:22–23 to discover the healthy character traits the Spirit's presence produces.

Every day presents me with numerous opportunities to follow either the flesh's natural tendencies or the Spirit's supernatural guidance. God's plan is that I would seek Him each day through His Word and prayer, depending on His Spirit to guide my way. This is what Paul meant when he said twice (5:16 and 5:25), "Walk in the Spirit."

Holy Spirit, thank You for making my heart Your home upon my new birth. It's awesome and yet humbling to think that You are in me. I'm grateful for the fact that You will never leave nor forsake me and that You specialize in cleansing, sanctifying, and growing me into the likeness of Jesus. Please grant me the wisdom, guidance, power, and love that I need to honor and serve You fully today.

"This I say then, Walk in the Spirit, and ye shall not fulfil the lust of the flesh."

Galatians 5:16

DAY 57

EPHESIANS 1–3

The Glorious Magnitude of God's Saving Grace

OVERVIEW

Paul spent two years in Ephesus during his third missionary journey (likely AD 52–54), leading people to Jesus Christ and establishing a local church. (We read about it on Day 35 in Acts 18.) This is more time than he usually spent in one place, and God developed a thriving church there. The letter of Ephesians was written to this congregation, roughly eight years later, while Paul was imprisoned in Rome.

The first half of Ephesians is doctrinal in nature, while the second half is more practical. This is appropriate, since our beliefs ultimately drive our behavior. This first half (chapters 1–3) focuses on the blessings of salvation which have been provided to us by Christ's extraordinary grace, beginning at the cross and extending into eternity.

APPLICATION

We need to be reminded of how fantastic the miracle of our salvation truly is. When we consider the great lengths to which God went in order to redeem our souls, it's truly humbling. "We have redemption through his blood" (1:7). I'm ashamed to say I have become so familiar with these truths that sometimes I'm guilty of reading verses like that and zoning out—daydreaming, even yawning.

We need to be reminded of the awesome greatness of God's master plan for our salvation. And Ephesians 1–3 lays that plan out in beautiful, rich terms. It begins and ends with God's grace, and we're the objects of that grace. Amazing grace, indeed!

- We were "dead in sin" but now we're alive in Christ (2:1).
- We were "children of wrath" but now we're objects of God's great love (2:3).

- We were "far off" and away from God but now we have been brought near to his heart (2:13).
- We were "strangers" but now we're members of his family (2:19).

Not only should it make us humble, but it should also make us grateful. We were lost rebels marching toward Hell, and He rescued us. Not only have we been delivered from eternal suffering, but we're bound for eternal joy and blessedness: "That in the ages to come he might shew the exceeding riches of his grace in his kindness toward us through Christ Jesus" (2:7). All of this, because of God's glorious grace and miraculous mercy.

Reminders like these are one reason we need to be in the Word daily. They help us worship the Lord and rejoice in His magnanimous grace.

Lord Jesus, I could never thank You enough for what You did to save my soul. By Your grace I'm saved. I could never have saved myself; it's Your gift. I did nothing to deserve it, so I won't ever boast about it. Thank You not only for dying for me and forgiving me, but for the countless things You have done, which have come along with my salvation. May my life bring You the glory You deserve, and may You use me to introduce others to You.

"For by grace are ye saved through faith; and that not of yourselves: it is the gift of God: Not of works, lest any man should boast."

Ephesians 2:8–9

DAY 58

EPHESIANS 4–6

How Christians Live—in the Church, at Home, at Work, and in the World

OVERVIEW

The second half of Ephesians is intensely practical, as Paul applies the gospel and grace to several areas of the believer's life. First, Paul speaks of unity, health, and growth in the local church (4:1–16). Then, he describes what growth and sanctification look like in several areas of an individual's life (4:17–5:21). Finally, Paul turns his attention to relationships between husbands and wives (5:22–33), children and parents (6:1–4), and those in the workplace (6:5–9). Paul closes his letter with a vivid appeal to be on the defensive against the spiritual attacks of the enemy by being clad in the armor God has provided us (6:10–20).

APPLICATION

Hands down, the four verses I have resorted to more often than any other when addressing relationship difficulty—in my own life and in pastoral counseling—are Ephesians 4:29–32. They clearly speak to where we all live, don't they? In the twenty-first century, our human relationships still face essentially the same threats and frustrations as in the first century.

God's instructions in these verses deal first with our words: "no corrupt communication." What if we adopted a policy of no name-calling, no sarcasm, no threats, and no hurtful language? God's rules for our words are that they be "edifying" (build up the listener) and that they give "grace" (be better than the listener has earned). Adopting these guidelines in our speech would immediately improve most relationships.

Then God says, "bitterness, wrath, anger, clamour (yelling), and malice (spitefulness)" are off-limits. Wouldn't any relationship benefit from the keeping out of these toxic poisons? Perhaps you've heard the wise saying, "Bitterness is the poison we swallow hoping to harm the one who offended us."

Ephesians 4:32 says, "And be ye kind one to another, tenderhearted…" The idea here is that we demonstrate these traits not only when they come easy, but precisely when we're tempted to be the opposite—unkind and hard-hearted—because we have been wronged. Notice the rest of the verse says, "forgiving one another, even as God for Christ's sake hath forgiven you." Ruth Bell Graham famously said, "A happy marriage is the union of two good forgivers." This truth applies to every relationship.

Every Christian has relationships in his or her life—at work, home, school, or church. Let's not let these instructions from Ephesians 4 fall on deaf ears. Let's sweeten and strengthen our relationships by following the wise instructions of our Heavenly Father.

Lord, thank You for the precious people You have placed in my life. I acknowledge that they and their joy are as important to You as me and my joy. Please forgive me for being harsh, unkind, impatient, and unforgiving. May I learn from You and follow You, whose presence contributes to the health of the relationships You have given me.

"Let all bitterness, and wrath, and anger, and clamour, and evil speaking, be put away from you, with all malice: And be ye kind one to another, tenderhearted, forgiving one another, even as God for Christ's sake hath forgiven you."

Ephesians 4:31–32

DAY 59

PHILIPPIANS 1–2

Serving the Lord with Joy, Unity, and Faithfulness

OVERVIEW

The church in Philippi, the first church on European soil, was founded during Paul's second missionary journey. This is the city where Lydia and the sorcerer slave-girl were saved, and where Paul and Silas were beaten and jailed, only to be miraculously released during the midnight earthquake when the jailer was converted (we read about this on Day 35).

Paul had quite the collection of memories with this body of believers, and he cherished these people. He wrote this letter to them from prison in Rome, several years after those missionary efforts. In spite of his imprisonment, the most commonly repeated terms in the book are *joy* or *rejoicing.* Paul had learned to find joy, not in his own shifting circumstances, but in God and in the good work God was accomplishing in the lives of others whom he loved.

APPLICATION

Philippians 2:5–11 contain some of the most crucial truths about the incarnation and exaltation of Jesus Christ in Scripture. And though the theology here is of infinite significance, there's also an example for believers to emulate practically.

In a passage where Paul was emphasizing our disposition toward other believers and promoting unity in the church (2:1–18), he said, to paraphrase verse 5, "Learn to think like Jesus did." Then he went on to describe three traits in Christ's incarnation:

- Servanthood: He "took upon him the form of a servant" (v. 7). If Jesus assumed the posture of a servant for me, then I should be willing to take on this posture toward others. Being a servant means submitting my interests, preferences, well-being, and opinions to those of another, prioritizing theirs above my own.

- Humility: "He humbled himself" (v. 8). Humility is the attitude that precedes the actions of a servant. By nature, I'm self-centered, but humility removes me from the center of my focus.
- Submission: He "became obedient unto death" (v. 8). The true test of servanthood is how you respond when you're treated like one. A true servant *submits* to the Lord, His Word, and those He has placed in authority. Pride rebels; humility submits.

Finally, verses 9–11 demonstrate that the Lord Jesus has been—and will be—highly exalted, in spite of His servanthood, humility, and submission.

The decision to serve others, humble myself, and submit to others requires faith. When every instinct inside me swells with self-importance and self-interest, it requires faith to take the humble approach. It requires faith that God Himself is watching, and that He will turn my submission and servanthood into my ultimate good, as He did so gloriously in the case of His Son.

Father, I confess that I tend to be proud and self-centered. Please crucify this fleshly behavior and replace it with the humility demonstrated by Your Son. Produce in me, by Your Spirit, an authentic servanthood and submission that You can bless and use. And may it cultivate harmony and joy within Your body, the church.

"But made himself of no reputation, and took upon him the form of a servant, and was made in the likeness of men: And being found in fashion as a man, he humbled himself, and became obedient unto death, even the death of the cross."

Philippians 2:7–8

DAY 60

PHILIPPIANS 3–4

Paul's Pursuit of Christ and His Gratitude for the Philippians

OVERVIEW

Paul cautions the Philippians concerning the same legalistic Judaizers who were troubling the churches in Galatia by attempting to add Jewish ceremonial laws to Christ's gospel. He goes on to describe his personal testimony of "reaching forth" to what God has for his life. He expresses gratitude for the numerous times the Philippians had sent financial support for his missionary endeavors, including their most recent gift, delivered by Epaphroditus, who had now returned to Philippi with this letter in hand. He also includes a handful of greetings and admonitions.

APPLICATION

The Christian life is a continuous journey, requiring forward motion. We never arrive, and we must never let up. Yes, there are seasons and ebbs and flows. But mostly it's about enduring, faithfully pursuing Christ and His image and advancing the glory of God. The New Testament indicates that the Christian life requires the endurance of a marathon runner, the patient toil of a farmer, the toughness of a soldier, and the diligent labor of a builder.

Paul's testimony in 3:13–14 follows this theme. He says, in essence, "I haven't arrived. But I'm not focused on the past; I'm focused on the future. I'm straining and stretching for the good things God has in store for me as I pursue Him and His plan for my life." Paul wasn't melancholy over his disappointments. Or satisfied over his accomplishments. Or bitter toward those who had betrayed him. Or complacent with his level of usefulness to God.

If we are looking for excuses to coast, drift, or quit the Christian life, we'll find them. Fatigue, disappointments, failures, and disillusionment threaten us all. That's why we need to draw inspiration from the pages of Scripture and especially from testimonies like Paul's. Make his testimony yours! Decide, "I'm going to forget the past and passionately pursue what God has for my days ahead, by faith."

I guarantee, if God gives you breath tomorrow, it's because He has plans to bless you, enable you, equip you, strengthen you, guide you, glorify His Son in you, advance His purposes through you, and reward your faithful service to Him.

Father, it's humbling and encouraging to consider that just as You had a plan for Paul's life, You also have a plan for mine. Thank You. Please strengthen me as I reach toward the good and godly things You have before me. Thank You for giving me this day, and may I take steps forward by Your enabling grace.

"Brethren, I count not myself to have apprehended: but this one thing I do, forgetting those things which are behind, and reaching forth unto those things which are before, I press toward the mark for the prize of the high calling of God in Christ Jesus."

Philippians 3:13–14

DAY 61

COLOSSIANS 1–2

Christ's Supremacy and Sufficiency

OVERVIEW

This letter is a rare case for Paul in that it was written to a body of believers in a city where he had never been. He hadn't met these people, nor had he been the instrument God used to start this local church, as had been the case with those in Philippi and Ephesus.

The pastor in Colossae was a faithful man named Epaphras. He was probably saved in Ephesus during Paul's third missionary journey and returned to his hometown of Colossae, one hundred miles east of Ephesus, to plant a church. Epaphras was concerned that false teachers were beginning to threaten his congregation's faith, so he traveled all the way to Rome to visit the imprisoned Paul (possibly in a form of house arrest). Paul was eager to help by drafting this letter, under the guidance of the Spirit, and sending it back with Tychicus, while Epaphras stayed in Rome for an additional season.

APPLICATION

When the Christian life comes right down to it, it really is all about Jesus. So each day, it is incumbent upon us to reconnect with Him, reorient our hearts toward Him, reignite our love for Him, and rededicate our lives to Him. That's why our daily time in fellowship with the Lord is so critical to our spiritual vitality. Think about it...in these two small chapters alone, we are reminded:

- He shed His blood for our forgiveness (1:14).
- He is God (1:15).
- He is the One and only Creator (1:16).
- His glory and pleasure are the purposes for all creation (1:16).
- He is the Head of the church, of which we are members (1:18).
- He possesses supreme authority over every realm (2:10).

- He took the shame, pain, and wrath that belonged to each of us, by carrying each and every one of our individual sins to His cross (2:14).
- He defeated Satan and evil, once and for all, by His death and resurrection (2:15).

Because of all this, He alone should "have the preeminence" (1:18) in the church, as well as in our hearts, minds, choices, priorities, values, words, schedules, affections, and loyalties.

For too many of us, Jesus lives on the *periphery* of our lives. But because of who He is and what He's done, Jesus is truly worthy of—and we should freely and purposefully give Him—the *preeminence.*

Lord Jesus, I praise You and acknowledge You as God alone. As Creator, Sustainer, Head, and Sovereign, I gladly bow my heart to You and yield my life to You. Thank You for, as Colossians 2:14 says, blotting out the handwriting of ordinances that was against me, which was contrary to me, and taking it out of the way, nailing it to Your cross. I invite You to be the center of my focus today. May I think, speak, and act in a way that demonstrates You are truly preeminent—the central feature—in my life.

"And he is the head of the body, the church: who is the beginning, the firstborn from the dead; that in all things he might have the preeminence."

Colossians 1:18

DAY 62

COLOSSIANS 3–4

Living in Light of Heaven

OVERVIEW

Paul helps the Colossians understand what it means for believers to live with eternity in view (3:1–2). It involves "putting off" old behaviors (3:5–11) and "putting on" a new set of behaviors (3:12–17). Simple, practical instructions follow concerning life's various relationships (3:18–4:1). Then Paul gives several greetings, from which we can learn about the character of some wonderful colaborers in Paul's service to the Lord.

APPLICATION

Becoming a Christian changes everything—at least, it should. A person's decision to believe in Christ doesn't only alter his future destination, but it also alters his present manner of living.

Paul explains that being born again should recalibrate what we pursue. "Seek those things which are above" (3:1)—i.e., that which matters in Heaven. So much of our daily routines tend to be earthbound in focus and results. We must become more conscious to this, learning to shift gears and give greater attention to those things which influence eternity.

Paul also says we should "set our affection" on things that matter in Heaven (3:2). My *affection* refers to what's important to me—what's getting the first priority in my investments of time, resources, and energy. Whatever has my affection is what occupies my thoughts, what I work toward, and what motivates me daily.

So take inventory. Where are your affections placed? What are you seeking? Is it primarily earthly things, such as your next possession, amusement, pleasure, promotion, or entertaining experience?

Let's recalibrate. Why not focus instead on the next prayer to be prayed, child to be raised, verse to be memorized, soul to be won, church project to be completed, hurting individual to be comforted, believer to be mentored, or word of kindness to be given?

Some have said that it's possible to be "so heavenly minded that you're no earthly good." But when we are truly heavenly minded, we are of *greater* earthly good. Focusing on eternity causes us to live here and now with an active sense of calling to God's purposes and service to others for His glory. In fact, my experience has been that there are far more believers, who are "so earthly minded that they're no heavenly good." That's the greater tragedy.

Lord, help me take inventory of my affections, in real time. Help me become more conscious of the eternal value of where my time, energy, and resources go. And may I adjust my life's investments in a way that more fully reflects Your priorities. Thank You for saving my soul, forgiving my sin, and preparing for me a home in Heaven. Help me to be more mindful of where I'm headed.

"If ye then be risen with Christ, seek those things which are above, where Christ sitteth on the right hand of God. Set your affection on things above, not on things on the earth."

Colossians 3:1–2

DAY 63

1 THESSALONIANS 1–3

A Diligent Missionary's Message to a Dynamic Congregation

OVERVIEW

Paul founded the church in Thessalonica during his second missionary journey. It was the second city reached with the gospel on the European continent (after Philippi) and was the largest city in its region. The gospel spread from Thessalonica throughout the Roman empire, due both to the city's strategic location along the Egnation Way and, more so, due to the vibrant witness of the believers.

This letter was one of Paul's earliest, written from Corinth later during that same journey and sent with Timothy. Paul sought to strengthen the new believers in the doctrines of the faith because he had left Thessalonica in a hurry due to persecution, unable to instruct the new believers as much as in other places. He also wrote to defend his character from the attacks of enemies, to communicate his love, and to express his concern for their spiritual well-being.

APPLICATION

Though the congregation in Thessalonica was young in the Lord, their faith was dynamic and growing. By the time Paul wrote this letter, their testimony was spreading throughout the empire. They didn't hide their faith, but allowed it to shine brightly. "For from you sounded out the word of the Lord not only in Macedonia and Achaia, but also in every place your faith to God-ward is spread abroad" (1:8).

There were two factors at work in their lives which are instructive for us:

- They *followed* the right example: "And ye became followers [imitators] of us" (1:6). One of God's key strategies in growing His children is the provision of mentors in the faith. Young Christians need spiritual leadership from mature believers, like newborn babies need the support and care of a family. If you have been disappointed by someone you admired, I encourage you, for your own sake, to resist the temptation to become cynical, guarded, and isolated. Our ultimate allegiance is to the Lord, but as we follow Him, it's His design that others encourage us along the way (Hebrews 10:24–25). Someone and some things are influencing you—so choose carefully who and what they are.

- They *provided* the right example: "So that ye were ensamples [literally, "patterns"] to all that believe" (1:7). Believers who benefit from following the right examples must eventually grow in maturity to the point that they pay it forward, providing a godly example for those coming behind them. I don't know what your exact role is in your local church, but I know you have influence, and God intends to use your life to positively impact others. Would your example encourage or discourage the faith of a new believer?

Lord, thank You that, in Your divine wisdom and plan for my life, You have placed godly influences around me, from whom I can benefit. Please reward their labor, in part by the fruit of my spiritual growth. And Lord, please use me as an encouragement to others. Make me a blessing through my words, attitudes, actions, and example. What a privilege, that I could be used by You to contribute to other believers' growth.

"Remembering without ceasing your work of faith, and labour of love, and patience of hope in our Lord Jesus Christ, in the sight of God and our Father;"

1 Thessalonians 1:3

DAY 64

1 THESSALONIANS 4–5

Living Sanctified Lives in Light of Christ's Return

OVERVIEW

Paul urges the Thessalonians to "walk the walk" of the Christian life by growing closer to the likeness of Christ and less like the world. Then he reminds them of the hopeful, exciting future return of Christ and the spirit of the age that will grow darker approaching that day. He finishes the letter with several staccato instructions for living fruitful lives as joyful believers.

APPLICATION

How do you view the relationship between a believer and his or her pastor? More importantly, how healthy is *your* relationship with *your* pastor? The Bible teaches that spiritual leaders are God's gifts to us for our spiritual growth and health (Ephesians 4:11). Paul wanted the believers in Thessalonica to get all that God intended out of their relationship with "them which labour among you, and are over you in the Lord" (5:12). So he gave them two simple commands:

- Know him (5:12). This means spending time under his influence, teaching, and preaching. It implies *learning* from him, and *leaning* into the relationship. The devil will surely seek to drive a wedge between a believer and his pastor, because he is aware of the importance of the relationship. Be guarded, and refuse to let that happen.
- Esteem him (5:13). This means treating his role with the respect it's due—not because of his greatness, but because of the greatness of the one who has called and assigned him. The writer of Hebrews says we should follow his faith (13:7). And as he speaks the truth and teaches the Word, we are to

"obey" (Hebrews 13:17) the instructions—not *his* instructions but the *Bible's* instructions which he delivers.

Warren Wiersbe wrote, "Spiritual leadership is a great responsibility and a difficult task. The battles and burdens are many, and sometimes the encouragements are few. It is dangerous when a church family takes their leaders for granted and fails to pray for them, work with them, and encourage them."

Lord Jesus, thank You for the spiritual influences You have placed in my life. Please enable me to get the most out of them by receiving Your Word, applying it to my life, and gleaning from their example and leadership. Please protect our relationship. And please protect my pastor in every way. May we serve You and glorify You together in harmony until Your return.

"And we beseech you, brethren, to know them which labour among you, and are over you in the Lord, and admonish you; And to esteem them very highly in love for their work's sake. And be at peace among yourselves."

1 Thessalonians 5:12–13

DAY 65

2 THESSALONIANS 1–3

Temporary Trouble for Believers, Ultimate Trouble for Unbelievers

OVERVIEW

Paul wrote this second letter to the same congregation in Thessalonica for a different purpose than the first, though the pastoral themes of nurture, encouragement, and instruction continue. False teachers once again threatened Paul's converts, this time with the notion that they had missed Christ's coming and were now living in the Tribulation. In the middle chapter of the letter, Paul explains that this had not occurred (it still hasn't), and provides detailed markers of what this event will look like, including the rise of Antichrist (2:8–9).

APPLICATION

Imagine if Paul were the missionary who brought you the gospel. How thrilling it would be to read in a letter from him, "We are bound to thank God always for you, brethren" (1:3). What made Paul so thankful for these believers who, though young in their faith, were an inspiration to others?

- They were growing: "your faith groweth exceedingly" (1:3). Regardless of how long you have been a Christian, it ought to be true that you're growing. We don't "arrive." There are likely some areas in which you used to struggle but no longer do. That's a testimony to growth. But what areas remain that need growth? Your prayer life? Your faithfulness in witnessing? Financial stewardship? Overcoming worry? Pride? Jealousy? Bitterness? Take your next step of growth!
- They were loving: "the charity of every one of you all toward each other aboundeth" (1:3) Are you loving toward your brothers and sisters in Christ? All of them? (Some are easy to love, others, not so easy.) What loving words

have you spoken to them? What loving actions have you extended in their direction recently?

- They were enduring: "your patience and faith in all your persecutions and tribulations that ye endure" (1:4). When you endure difficulty, people become thankful for you. Your pastor will thank God for your faithfulness. Your children, your spouse, and others you influence (the number is larger than you think) will be thankful that through life's unexpected twists and turns, you remained faithful. And they noticed. It inspires, encourages, and strengthens them.

As a pastor, I can't adequately express how thankful I am for people in our church who are growing, loving, and enduring. I might understand how Paul felt.

Lord, thank You for the people You have placed in my life, whom I have the privilege of observing, who are growing in their faith, loving in their actions, and enduring in their trials. They are a true encouragement. Now please help me—I need Your grace—to grow, love, and endure.

"We are bound to thank God always for you, brethren, as it is meet, because that your faith groweth exceedingly, and the charity of every one of you all toward each other aboundeth; So that we ourselves glory in you in the churches of God for your patience and faith in all your persecutions and tribulations that ye endure:"

2 Thessalonians 1:3–4

DAY 66

1 TIMOTHY 1–3

Instructions, Exhortations, and Qualifications for Pastors

OVERVIEW

Paul's letters have so far been addressed to churches, but this one is addressed to an individual—Timothy. Timothy was saved as a young man, most likely during Paul's first missionary journey while in Lystra. After his conversion, Timothy grew spiritually to the point that he was invited to join the team during their second journey (Acts 16:1–3). After traveling with Paul extensively for some years, Timothy was called to lead the church in Ephesus. This letter contained Paul's instructions for the young pastor, providing him the mentoring needed to conduct a fruitful, faithful, and doctrinally-sound ministry.

APPLICATION

How would you respond if someone asked you whether the gospel of Jesus Christ is *inclusive* or *exclusive*? Verses 4–6 in chapter 2 provide the answer.

Paul, through the inspiration of the Holy Spirit, says in 2:4 that it is God's desire for "all men to be saved" by coming to know the truth. Then, in 2:6, he says that Christ gave Himself "for all." Apparently, the gospel is *inclusive,* because all people are invited. After all, the word *gospel* means "good news" and that's only true if it's inclusive. Anyone from anywhere, with any background, having committed any sin, from any nationality, of any skin color, carrying any baggage, can receive the good news that is the gospel. That's awesome! This good news is that we can be rescued from the eternal consequences of our sin and be given a relationship with our Creator God because of His Son Jesus' sacrifice on the cross, on our behalf. That's inclusive!

But it's also *exclusive.* The God who invites all, says that they may come to Him by only one means—the "door" of Jesus Christ (John 10:9). Chapter 2 verse 5 states, "For there is one God, and one mediator between God and men, the man Christ Jesus."

There's simply no other way. So it's exclusive. It's narrow. Jesus Himself said that He is "the way" (John 14:6) to the Father—not one of many ways. Salvation is not found in any other name (Acts 4:12).

If I invite you into my home, I will direct you on how to enter. If you try to come through the wall, windows, or roof, you won't be successful. You must come through the door. But the important thing is, you're invited!

We live in a world where the culture is confused and where tolerance is valued over truth. What this world needs are Christians who clearly and compassionately communicate that Christ "gave himself a ransom for all" (2:6) and that He is truly the "one mediator between God and men" (2:5). In a world literally dying for answers, may we not be silent.

Lord Jesus, thank You for including me in Your plan of salvation! Thank You for giving Yourself for all mankind on the cross. Please help the people who live and work around me to understand what You have done for them, and please use me as Your witness in helping them know that You are a truly wonderful Saviour and the only way to God.

"Who will have all men to be saved, and to come unto the knowledge of the truth. For there is one God, and one mediator between God and men, the man Christ Jesus; Who gave himself a ransom for all, to be testified in due time."

1 Timothy 2:4–6

DAY 67

1 TIMOTHY 4–6

Practical Instructions for Biblical Living

OVERVIEW

In the second half of his letter, Paul instructs Timothy on how to deal with false teachers and also how to tend to his own spiritual health and testimony. He provides guidance on how the church cares for widows and compensates pastors. He spends much of the final chapter focused on how Timothy may help people learn to correctly view financial resources and material possessions.

APPLICATION

The message of 1 Timothy 6:6–18, on money and materialism, is more needed today than in any time of history. Though the resources at the average person's disposal today would boggle the mind of the first-century resident of the Middle East, the human tendency toward materialism and selfishness existed then as it does today.

These verses instruct us that we must learn contentment (6:6–8). Sadly, the discontented individual is never satisfied, on a continual treadmill of sorts, ever reaching for the next item, never able to enjoy that which was grasped yesterday. We must come to see this tendency in ourselves.

We should also learn from the tragedies that materialism and the unbridled pursuit of money has caused others—people who have lost what's truly valuable (relationships, ethics, quality of life) in their misguided chase for material wealth (6:9–10). Instead of pursuing things, we must learn to pursue what God values—godly character, faithfulness, and that which is eternally significant (6:11–12).

God's great antidote for materialism and discontent is generosity (6:17–18). Those who have been blessed—which clearly includes you and me—must learn to be conduits of blessing, through which financial resources flow to bless others. We must be careful to avoid placing our trust in those resources or finding our satisfaction in those resources, instead willingly distributing those resources to others.

This is the truly wealthy man—the one who recognizes all he has comes from God, the one who determines to be "rich in good works," and the one who becomes joyfully generous toward others.

Lord, thank You for providing so generously for me. I confess that often times my attention is directed toward the gifts You give instead of the Giver who provides them. Please forgive me for that. Help me learn and practice contentment. And make me a blessing to others by cultivating a generous spirit in me that willingly distributes to others and faithfully gives back to You.

"But godliness with contentment is great gain. For we brought nothing into this world, and it is certain we can carry nothing out. And having food and raiment let us be therewith content."

1 Timothy 6:6–8

DAY 68

2 TIMOTHY 1–4

Paul's Legacy and His Philosophy of Pastoral Ministry

OVERVIEW

Paul's last letter (chronologically) is also his most personal. He starts by recalling Timothy's heritage of faith on his mother's side. He expresses what it means to be unashamed of Christ and challenges Timothy to be strong in the face of difficulty and doctrinal confusion. He forecasts the failing moral conditions of the "last days" in which we are now living. And he closes the letter by reflecting on his faithful legacy in ministry, passing the baton of gospel preaching to his "son in the faith."

APPLICATION

As a pastor, I cherish the contents of Paul's second letter to Timothy, and the opening verses of chapter 2 is one of my favorite sections. These little-but-critical instructions are for all believers, not just pastors. Notice five commands given in these verses:

- Be strong (v. 1). This is not referring to physical strength or mere personal discipline. We are to be strong *in grace*. Grace is God's divine enabling. It's our only hope for being strong enough for what life throws at us, and it's only available through an abiding relationship with Christ.
- Teach truth (v. 2). This is how the gospel extends through each generation. Timothy must teach people what he has learned, and these people are to then teach others. This equation includes you and me. It doesn't stop with missionaries (like Paul) or pastors (like Timothy). It requires that each link in the chain of gospel advancement passes on the truth to the next.
- Endure hardness (v. 3). The metaphor of verse 3 is a soldier, because after all, we are in a war (Ephesians 6). We must not quit or surrender when following Christ leads to hard seasons.

- Please Christ (v. 4). Paul says the way to avoid becoming entangled in this world's traps is by keeping our eyes focused on pleasing Christ—the One who is the motivation for every spiritual decision and the aim of every act of service.
- Strive lawfully (v. 5). This term is borrowed from the Greek and Olympic games. It means to "play by the rules." If Timothy was to cross the finish line of his life and ministry well, as Paul was about to, he must not cut corners or make compromises. He must be obedient to the Word and the Spirit.

These five imperatives are vital. Take inventory, then take action.

Lord Jesus, I desire to please You on this journey. But I know I cannot succeed without the strength of Your grace. So please provide it day by day. Strengthen me to endure hardness as I keep my focus on You. Grant me opportunities to teach truth. And help me walk in step with Your Word so that I may "finish my course with joy" as Paul did.

"Thou therefore endure hardness, as a good soldier of Jesus Christ. No man that warreth entangleth himself with the affairs of this life; that he may please him who hath chosen him to be a soldier."

2 Timothy 2:3–4

DAY 69

TITUS 1–3

Encouraging a Pastor as He Equips Churches for Gospel Ministry

OVERVIEW

This letter to Titus, along with the two to Timothy, comprise what we refer to as the Pastoral Epistles. Like Timothy, Titus was one of Paul's sons in the faith (1:4), likely saved during the first missionary journey, later serving as a co-laborer (2 Corinthians 7–8), and now pastoring in Crete, a place where Paul had pioneered a work for Christ's kingdom. The young churches on this Mediterranean island were in need of being stabilized and having pastors trained and appointed to lead them. Paul writes to provide qualifications for those pastors, to warn against false teaching, to provide instructions for Christian living, and to encourage Titus personally.

APPLICATION

Someone once asked me, "What is grace?" I provided a simple answer, gave an illustration or two, quoted a few scriptures, and—most importantly—explained the gospel. But the doctrine of God's grace is deeper and more awesome than one conversation could possibly express.

We know that grace is God's undeserved favor toward us. We know that it provides salvation to all who come to God by faith through Christ (3:7). But grace doesn't stop with the miracle of salvation—although that alone is amazing enough!

Grace also includes the supernatural work of God within us, by way of His Spirit, progressively transforming us into the image of Christ until our arrival in Heaven. His grace provides strength during weak moments, comfort during painful moments, and escape during tempting moments.

In today's passage, Paul tells Titus that grace "teaches" us some things (2:11–12). What does grace teach us? It teaches us to "deny ungodliness and worldly lusts," to "live soberly, righteously, and godly" (2:12), to look for Christ's appearing (2:13), and to become a people who are "zealous of good works" (2:14).

Occasionally, a misinformed believer will claim that God's grace grants us a free pass to live in whatever manner we wish, even recklessly, carelessly, and sinfully. But Paul believed (and God wants us to know) that grace teaches us—it trains, motivates, mentors us—to live free from the sin that characterizes our fallen world, to live in anticipation of Christ's return, and to live a life that's filled with good works.

"Good works" are a theme in this letter (2:7,14; 3:1,8,14). God's plan is that these good works characterize His people, serving as a testimony to the authenticity of the gospel they share with their neighbors.

Lord, thank You for Your grace. I praise You and thank You for saving me by grace and for activating Your grace in my life so that I might become more like Your Son. Help me learn from Your grace. Help me apply its reality to every part of my life—my thoughts, words, attitudes, actions, choices, and more. Make me a shining light for You, whose good works and gospel witness work together to point people to the saving knowledge of Your wonderful Son!

"Who gave himself for us, that he might redeem us from all iniquity, and purify unto himself a peculiar people, zealous of good works."

Titus 2:14

DAY 70

PHILEMON

Forgiveness and Restoration for a Runaway Slave

OVERVIEW

Like other areas of first-century life, the issue of slavery must be understood in its historical context. Slavery was, during that time, very different than the abhorrent system of slavery we think of in American and European history. No brand of slavery is approved in God's eyes; it was, nonetheless, part of the structure of a fallen society in which first-century believers found themselves. With approximately one-third of Roman residents holding the status of a slave, including working-class professionals such as doctors, teachers, and accountants, a slave's standard of living was often higher than free men, since they were provided for by their masters. Bible writers never condoned slavery. They expressed the spiritual equality of slave and master (Galatians 3:28, Ephesians 6:9, Colossians 4:1, 1 Timothy 6:1–2, Philemon 16) and sought to end the abuses involved in the arrangement by changing people's hearts.

Philemon, the recipient of Paul's shortest letter, was a wealthy slave owner. It is likely that he received Christ in Ephesus, during Paul's second missionary journey. He later became an involved member of the church in Colossae. The subject of this letter is Onesimus, a slave who had stolen money from Philemon and fled to Rome. As only God's providence could have allowed, Paul had the joy of leading Onesimus to Christ. Paul sent this letter back to Philemon, in the hands of Onesimus, instructing Philemon to forgive Onesimus and restore him to fellowship as a brother. So Tychicus and Onesimus travelled to Colossae together, Tychicus carrying the church's letter and Onesimus this letter to Philemon, a member of that church.

APPLICATION

I have often wondered how the scene unfolded when Onesimus hand-delivered this letter to his former master, Philemon. Was it awkward for them both? Philemon never expected to see Onesimus again. Why would a runaway slave return? Was Philemon immediately receptive to Paul's instruction to extend forgiveness? I'm sure it all worked out beautifully, but the greater lesson for us is found in the message of forgiveness. We have all been in Philemon's shoes—someone had wronged us and now seeks forgiveness. How do we respond?

The entire scenario was ultimately affected by one major fact—Onesimus had been saved (vv. 10–11)! The gospel changes everything. Philemon needed to remember that he too had once been a sinner in need of God's forgiveness—just like Onesimus. He and Onesimus had far more in common now than they had before.

Forgiveness requires grace—treating people better than they deserve (just as we have been treated by God). Paul said, "Receive him for ever; Not now as a servant, but above a servant, a brother beloved" (vv. 15–16). This is the disposition God calls us to demonstrate toward those we forgive. We don't hold it over their heads or seek vengeance or remind them of their failure. Instead, we give grace.

The greatest motivation to forgive is found in Christ. Check out the words of Paul to Philemon in verses 18–19, and hear them as the words of Jesus to you when He calls on you to forgive someone. Don't forgive them because they're worthy; forgive them because Christ is worthy, and because of what He's done for you.

Lord Jesus, thank You for extending grace and forgiveness to me. Thank You for taking all of my sins and placing them on Your account on the cross. I owe You my very life for time and eternity. If there's someone I'm holding bitterness toward right now, I commit to release it. Please enable me to give the grace to others that You have so generously given to me.

"If he hath wronged thee, or oweth thee ought, put that on mine account;"

Philemon 18

DAY 71

HEBREWS 1–2

Jesus Is Greater, Higher, and Better Than the Angels

OVERVIEW

The book of Hebrews is actually a letter, like so many of the New Testament books. But this is the only one whose writer is unknown. It could have been Paul, Barnabas, Silas, Luke, or someone else. But even though we don't know who the human author was, we *do* know that the ultimate author was the Holy Spirit, as with all biblical books (2 Peter 1:21).

Hebrews (as the name begins to imply) compares Jesus Christ and His Gospel to the Jewish Old Covenant worship, involving the Temple, the priesthood, the animal sacrifices, and the ceremonies. The theme of the book is that, in every way, Jesus is *better* (1:4, 7:22). Because of its anonymous nature, there are few personal references compared to other epistles. What it does contain, however, is rich imagery that expresses the greatness and glory of our wonderful Saviour.

APPLICATION

The name of Jesus is precious to us who know Him. But our grasp of His greatness is sometimes lost in our familiarity with Him. To know Him is to love Him. But as with other relationships, to know Him over time can also be to take Him for granted. Hebrews is the right prescription for this condition. Consider Hebrews 1:3.

Jesus is "the brightness of his glory." This expresses our God's awesomeness and ultimate holiness. Higher and holier and more glorious than we have ever experienced or anything we could imagine. That's our Saviour.

Jesus is "the express image of his person." Before, during, and after His incarnation, Jesus was and is God. During His thirty-three years of life on this earth, He was God in the flesh, literally, fully, and completely.

Jesus upholds "all things by the word of his power." The solar system, our human bodies, Earth's orbit, the laws of nature and science—all of them depend on His power. His spoken word possesses that kind of authority.

Jesus "by himself purged our sins." To purge our sin is to take it away, remove it, cleanse it, and completely do away with its effects. It cost Him His life on the cross. And He did it for you and me.

Jesus has sat "down on the right hand of the Majesty on high." As the divine plan for our redemption unfolded, He rose from the grave, ascended to Heaven, and is seated on His heavenly throne. Governments, kingdoms, religions, cults, and ideological movements may think they're making progress toward overthrowing His authority, but in the end He has the last laugh (Psalm 2:1–4).

This is our Saviour! The one to whom we pray, the one we follow, the one we witness of, the one who is our ever-present companion, and before whom we will one day stand. Let's be reminded and encouraged about the greatness of Jesus!

Lord Jesus, I praise You for who You are, and for what You have done. Thank You for allowing me to have a relationship with You because of Your sacrifice on the cross and Your grace toward me. I'm humbled by it. Help me stay mindful throughout the day of Your greatness and goodness.

"Who being the brightness of his glory, and the express image of his person, and upholding all things by the word of his power, when he had by himself purged our sins, sat down on the right hand of the Majesty on high;"

Hebrews 1:3

DAY 72

HEBREWS 3–4

Jesus Is Better Than Moses; His Rest Is Better Than the Sabbath

OVERVIEW

Moses was the most revered figure in Jewish history, but the writer of Hebrews demonstrates that Jesus is even better than Moses. He also likens our salvation to the entering of the Promised Land; that is, it can be entered only by faith. Unbelief leaves us on the outside. In chapter 4 we learn about the rest Jesus provides. The rest provided through a daily relationship with Him is better than the rest the Hebrews received, one day per week on the Sabbath. Yes, Jesus is better!

APPLICATION

Our focus on Jesus continues in today's reading. All that is said about Him rises to a crescendo in the final three verses (4:14–16).

He is our "great high priest" whose ministry isn't limited to an earthly tabernacle or temple. His priestly ministry is carried out in "the heavens" (v. 14) where He ministers on our behalf as He reigns. What a Saviour!

He has been "touched with the feeling of our infirmities," (v. 15) which means the pains and stresses, the burdens and temptations we feel, He Himself faced during His earthly ministry. We will never carry a feeling of heaviness that He hasn't carried Himself. When no one else knows how you feel, He does.

And when it comes to temptation with sin, Jesus passed that test as no man ever has, before or since. He was utterly and completely "without sin" in spite of being "in all points tempted like as we are" (v. 15). So, the battles you and I face today, He has already won.

In light of all of this about Jesus, there is one obvious response for every child of God, "Let us therefore come boldly unto the throne of grace, that we may obtain mercy, and find grace to help in time of need" (v. 16).

Since He is our heavenly, enthroned Priest who knows everything we face and has conquered every temptation, let's run to Him. Let's enter His throne room each and every day. Let's seek Him and request the mercy and grace we need for each and every one of our needs. And let's do it boldly—with every confidence that He stands ready, willing, and able.

Lord Jesus, I praise You for Your high and holy position in Heaven. I bow my heart and head in reverence to You. Thank You for coming to earth in such a way that allowed You to feel every pain and face every temptation I will ever feel or face. I'm thankful that You truly understand. Please grant me the mercy and grace needed to meet each of my needs.

"Let us therefore come boldly unto the throne of grace, that we may obtain mercy, and find grace to help in time of need."

Hebrews 4:16

DAY 73

HEBREWS 5–7

Jesus Our High Priest Is Better Than the Levitical Priesthood

OVERVIEW

Simply put, a priest is a go-between (a mediator) between mankind and God. Throughout Jewish history, selected men from the tribe of Levi served in this capacity at the Temple. But Jesus is presented in Hebrews as our great high priest (4:15) of the New Testament. He is the one final Priest through whom every believer may come to God. But Jesus wasn't from the tribe of Levi; He was a descendant of Judah.

Jesus' priesthood extends back past Levi—and past Aaron, the specific Levite from whose descendants the priests came. Jesus' priesthood not only stretches into eternity future, a "high priest for ever" (6:20), but also extends back to a mysterious priest who met Abraham hundreds of years before Levi and Aaron, the priest Melchisedec. This priest was a foreshadowing (a "type") of the one great eternal Priest who would one day come—fulfilled in Jesus. Many believe Melchisedec may have been a supernatural Old Testament appearance of Christ, a *theophany*. In either case, the message of Hebrews is, that Jesus Christ is our one and final mediator. And this is better than attempting to gain access to God through Levite priests, imperfect human beings.

APPLICATION

Would you assess yourself as being a "strong" Christian? How about "mature?" Our tendency is to overestimate our spiritual health and development. Apparently it was the tendency of the recipients of the letter of Hebrews as well. Because there's a corrective challenge given by the writer in 5:12–14. In his diagnosis, some believers have truths and principles to learn that they not only should already have mastered, but should by now be teaching to others (5:12). He blames their condition on two things.

First, they hadn't become skillful in the word (5:13). These people weren't rolling up their sleeves and digging into the Scriptures the way God intended. They knew the basics, but their scriptural understanding was only on the surface. They needed to find their way around God's Word, diving deeper than simple platitudes and cliché anecdotes. Like an explorer, they needed to search wider and deeper with greater diligence.

Second, they hadn't exercised their sense of discernment (5:14). They weren't putting the Word into action. They weren't exercising discernment. They weren't making decisions or choices based on Scripture, and they weren't scrutinizing life's issues through the lens of Scripture.

Am I a strong, mature Christian? I guess the answer is revealed by whether I am diligently digesting the Word of God (like meat), and whether I am exercising Bible-driven discernment in each area of my life. How about you?

Heavenly Father, Thank You for giving me Your Word. I long to be a more diligent student of it. Grant me understanding from Your Spirit as I read, hear, and study it. Help me to apply it to my life correctly, and help me learn to see life through it. May Your Word shape my thinking, my actions, and my words.

"For every one that useth milk is unskilful in the word of righteousness: for he is a babe. But strong meat belongeth to them that are of full age, even those who by reason of use have their senses exercised to discern both good and evil."

Hebrews 5:13–14

DAY 74

HEBREWS 8–10

Our High Priest Also Became Our Once-for-All Sacrifice for Sin

OVERVIEW

The theme of Jesus as our High Priest continues into today's reading. But the description of our Saviour's role is developed significantly further. During the Old Testament period, the priests brought sacrifices daily, but their offerings could not satisfy the spiritual debt that sin accumulated. So the following day, incomplete offerings would be brought by imperfect priests, once again. And so the cycle went. Until the once-for-all Saviour, the Lord Jesus Christ as the perfect divine High Priest who had no sins of His own, brought the ultimate sacrifice—Himself. And this sacrifice would not merely be brought into the holy place of the Tabernacle or Temple but would be carried all the way into Heaven. With this one final payment for sin, our sins and iniquities will be remembered by God no more (8:12 and 10:17)—if we receive Him.

APPLICATION

I hope as you read of what Jesus Christ has done for us, especially in contrast to the insufficient sacrificial system under which the Jews operated during the Old Covenant, that your heart swells with gratitude and wonder. What a wonderful Saviour, not only to make the sacrifice of His own life, but to devise before time the means by which our awful sins could be forgiven.

This truth must be received. Have you personally *received* Jesus Christ as your Saviour? We sometimes call this being *saved* or *born again* (a term Jesus coined). It's a decision. Have you made it?

After we have received Christ, we must *respond* to the truth of what He has done for us. In response to the awesome sacrifice Jesus has made for us, the writer of Hebrews suggests three responses to this wonderful reality of forgiveness and redemption. These are signaled by the expression, "Let us…" (10:22–25).

Draw closer. "Let us draw near with a true heart" (v. 22). May we draw closer to God. Think of what He has done for us! He has invited us into an ever-deepening personal relationship with Him.

Stand strong. "Let us hold fast the profession of our faith without wavering" (v.23). May we stand strong for God. Let's not cave in to temptation or pressure to forsake our Saviour's will, words, or ways. May we be loyal, true, and faithful.

Encourage others. "And let us consider one another to provoke unto love and to good works: Not forsaking the assembling of ourselves together" (vv. 24–25). May we encourage others toward God. Let's band together as an assembly of blood-bought believers who, in spite of all our differences, find a glorious common bond in our gracious and merciful Saviour.

What will you do with what you have received? How will you respond?

Lord Jesus, thank You for not only serving as my faithful and sinless High Priest, for which I praise You, but also for laying down Your own life for the cleansing of my sin. I owe You my life. As I attempt to draw near to You, I trust Your promise that You will draw near to me (James 4:8). Please strengthen me and use me to encourage others in their walk with You along the way.

"Let us hold fast the profession of our faith without wavering; (for he is faithful that promised;) And let us consider one another to provoke unto love and to good works:"

Hebrews 10:23–24

DAY 75

HEBREWS 11–13

Living a Life of Faith and Faithfulness toward God

OVERVIEW

Chapter 11 defines *faith* and then articulates several examples of what was accomplished "by faith" in the lives of both well-known and little-known Old Testament characters. Against the backdrop of this "cloud of witnesses" (12:1) who have gone before us, we too can live faithfully and by faith. We can endure chastening (12:5–11), live out our faith in practical terms, follow spiritual leadership (13:7,17), and go the distance in our Christian lives. We can do all these and more, carried along by our faith in God.

APPLICATION

The basic message that follows the cataloging of the "hall of faith" in chapter 11, is "don't quit!" Because of a faithful God, don't quit. Because others have proven Him faithful, don't quit. The writer of Hebrews was concerned that some of his readers would "be wearied and faint in your minds" (12:3). But we can be faithful, if we simply keep faith in Him. Three elements emerge in 12:1–3:

- The race to run (12:1): As in other passages, our lives are likened to a race. It's a marathon, not a sprint, so we must run with patience. Endurance is required. Uphill terrain will be involved. We must put out of our minds the notion that we're entitled to a downhill stroll. No, this is a race. But we're not in competition with one another; we each have a course to run that is uniquely our own, "set before us."
- The obstacles to overcome (12:1): The first obstacle that will derail our race is *weights*, "let us lay aside every weight." The second obstacle is *wrongdoing*, "the sin which doth so easily beset us." These barnacle-like items attach to our lives and constrict our ability to pursue our race with the energy and swiftness God

intends. The third obstacle, which emerges over time is *weariness*, "lest ye be wearied and faint in your minds" (12:3).

- The example to follow (12:2): "Looking unto Jesus." Jesus didn't quit, though He faced a more challenging, grueling, painful set of circumstances than any of us ever will. His death and resurrection are living proof that God specializes in turning horrible stories into wonderful endings. That happy ending is ours—if we don't quit.

I'm not sure what burden you're bearing today or what trial you're enduring. But I do know that the solution is looking to Jesus from wherever you are. Not only will His example inspire you, but—even more importantly—His presence will strengthen and enable you to go forward, by faith.

Lord Jesus, I praise You for the amazing endurance You demonstrated on the cross. And I thank You that You are involved in my life today. Sometimes I focus on the burdens, the issues of the day, or the world around me. But what I really need to do is look to You. And when I do, everything comes into perspective. You love me. You have a plan. And You are in control of every circumstance that surrounds me. I praise You for Your power and I thank You for exercising it on my behalf.

"Looking unto Jesus the author and finisher of our faith; who for the joy that was set before him endured the cross, despising the shame, and is set down at the right hand of the throne of God."

Hebrews 12:2

DAY 76

JAMES 1–2

How Genuine Faith Is Demonstrated in the Real World

OVERVIEW

There are four men named James in the New Testament. This book was written by James, the half-brother of Jesus (one of Joseph and Mary's children). This James was not an apostle, but was, of course, an eyewitness to the ministry of Jesus. Acts records his role as a pastoral leader in the first church in Jerusalem. He wrote this letter to Jewish believers in Christ, who had been scattered as a result of the rising persecution in Jerusalem.

Compared to other New Testament writers, James focuses a greater portion of his letter on behavior—the practical ways we live out our faith. Chapter 1 addresses perseverance in suffering, resisting temptation, and responding to the Word. Chapter 2 discusses the need for impartiality, then explains that authentic faith is accompanied by and demonstrated through works.

APPLICATION

James' book has been referred to as "the Proverbs of the New Testament" because it contains many direct, pithy statements concerning wise Christian living. Consider several practical encouragements contained in the first chapter:

- Trials and difficulties are a cause for joy, not grief, because by those experiences, God is at work in our lives to make us mature and maximize our usefulness (1:2–4).
- Wisdom is within the reach of a simple prayer—just ask (1:5).
- Resist temptation, because it will always take you further than you want to go and cost you more than you want to pay (1:12–15).
- Be slow to get angry, because anger never produces your desired outcome (1:19–20).

- The Bible isn't simply given to us to read. It's given to change us by applying what we read to our lives (1:22–25).
- Actions speak louder than words. If someone claims to be godly but can't control their speech, they're all talk (1:26).

Then, consider chapter 2. The primary lesson (2:14–26) is that "faith without works is dead" (2:26). But was James contradicting the message of Paul, who emphasized that justification is by faith, without works? No, there's no contradiction. There's a *clarification*. James clarifies that if someone's faith is authentic, it will produce good works. In this case, the works are not the means to salvation but the result of salvation. I have heard it said this way, "Faith alone saves; but the faith that saves is not alone."

Heavenly Father, I thank You for every good gift that has come down from You. As I compare my Christian character and daily behavior to the book of James, I discover that I have some work to do. I need to allow my faith and Your Word to transform my behavior in some specific ways. Please grant me the wisdom and grace that I need to live the transformed life that you intend.

"Pure religion and undefiled before God and the Father is this, To visit the fatherless and widows in their affliction, and to keep himself unspotted from the world."

James 1:27

DAY 77

JAMES 3–5

How God's People Relate to Others

OVERVIEW

The natural man doesn't tend to get along with those around him because he is prone to pride, jealousy, and selfishness by nature. But God's people can—and ought to—live differently. That's James' message here. We should consider our words, prefer others over ourselves, seek peace, humble our hearts, practice generosity, and exercise compassion. This kind of living is only derived from "the wisdom that is from above" (3:17).

APPLICATION

It has been said, "Attitude is a little thing that makes a big difference." That's true. And what's true about our attitude is also true about our words. As James takes aim at the believers' lives, the area to which he devotes the lengthiest section is the topic of our words.

We could summarize James 3:2–12 by saying, "Words are little things that make a big impact." Like little bits move great horses and little rudders steer great boats and little fires destroy great buildings, the tongue is a little thing that makes a great impact.

Have you stopped lately to consider the power of your words? The wisest man to ever live said, "Death and life are in the power of the tongue" (Proverbs 18:21). One of the greatest ways you influence those around you—family members, coworkers, neighbors, and fellow church members—is through your words. They are the primary tools with which you build—or destroy—relationships.

During a tour of the United States Capitol building, I was informed that George Washington prohibited those under his command from using the Lord's name in vain. He told the troops that it made no sense to ask for God's help in battle while at other times use His name in cursing. That's similar to the point James makes in 3:9. Bowing our heads to bless God, only to rise from prayer and curse men just doesn't make sense.

James says our words are like fountains that produce water or like trees that produce fruit (2:11–12). We must give attention that the words that flow from our hearts (Matthew 12:34–36) are not unkind, sarcastic, demeaning, harsh, or hurtful. Instead, they should be thoughtful, gracious, edifying, and encouraging.

If you're looking for a little way to make a big improvement in life's relationships, take inventory of the words you're using. They make a difference!

Lord God, I'm humbled—even ashamed—to consider that You hear every word I speak, regardless of the audience. Please forgive me for being so careless with such powerful weapons. Cleanse my fountain, I pray, all the way to my heart, where my words originate. Make me kind, sensitive, holy, and gracious—like You. Help me remember James' challenge. And grant me the guidance, wisdom, and strength to use my words as a greater force for good.

"Even so the tongue is a little member, and boasteth great things. Behold, how great a matter a little fire kindleth!"

James 3:5

DAY 78

1 PETER 1–2

Christian Living in the Face of Hostility

OVERVIEW

The Christians to whom Peter wrote were suffering. Among other causes, it's likely that their greatest persecution came as a result of Nero's false claim that Christians had burned Rome. The destruction of Rome in A.D. 64 was actually done by Nero himself. But he used the Christians as a scapegoat. And so an intense persecution commenced, especially for those living in the regions mentioned in 1:1.

Peter desired to encourage these suffering believers, so their faith would not falter. Chapter 1 seeks to refocus the believers' attention on the goodness of God, the reality of Heaven, and the security of the believer. Chapter 2 explains that we should view ourselves here on earth as pilgrims who don't belong, whose patient endurance will ultimately glorify God and vindicate our faith before this world's observers.

APPLICATION

If we pay attention, the rich language Peter uses to describe our relationship with Christ will encourage us and strengthen our faith. We have a "lively hope" (1:3) that's cause to "greatly rejoice" (1:6), regardless of difficult circumstances.

In fact, there are at least three things about our faith that are absolutely unaffected by difficulties, trials, or tragedies. You might say these things are "incorruptible," because God says so. The word *corruptible* means "perishable or able to decay." Three things are not, and that is awesome news!

- Heaven is incorruptible. "To an inheritance incorruptible, and undefiled, and that fadeth not away, reserved in heaven for you," (1:4). If life on earth becomes difficult, painful, and tragic, that simply has no bearing on your reservation in Heaven. No one or nothing can change the fact that you get to spend forever in a perfect place where there's no pain, suffering, disease, sin, or death.

- Jesus' blood is incorruptible. "Forasmuch as ye know that ye were not redeemed with corruptible things, as silver and gold...but with the precious blood of Christ" (1:18–19). The sacrifice of Jesus Christ cannot be taken away from you. No matter your failure or sin, His blood is enough!
- The Word of God is incorruptible. "Being born again, not of corruptible seed, but of incorruptible, by the word of God, which liveth and abideth for ever" (1:23). After all this time, the Bible still stands as a rock undaunted. His promises will be fulfilled and His truth cannot be altered.

Don't let cable news or life's stresses cause you to think that things are spinning out of control. Yes, our trials are real. But God does give us perspective to rejoice through them. If you're saved, maybe the most important reminders you need are that God's promises are unchanging, His blood is still applied to your account, and an eternity of joy awaits you.

Lord Jesus, I praise and thank You for the precious blood that You shed for me as a Lamb without blemish. Thank You for Your forever reliable Word. And thank You for the reservation in Heaven waiting for me, earned not by my works but by Your perfect merit. What an assurance is mine! May I endure whatever You have for me, by Your grace, in a manner that reflects those realities.

"Forasmuch as ye know that ye were not redeemed with corruptible things, as silver and gold, from your vain conversation received by tradition from your fathers; But with the precious blood of Christ, as of a lamb without blemish and without spot:"

1 Peter 1:18–19

DAY 79

1 PETER 3–5

Perspective and Counsel on Suffering

OVERVIEW

As Peter continues to counsel those living in the midst of a society that opposes them, he addresses marriage. What if your spouse, of all people, opposes you as an unbeliever? Peter's answer is to be a gracious, spiritually-authentic Christian and to allow your testimony to win your spouse to Christ (3:1–7). He also encourages grace and hospitality among the believers so that we might encourage one another along the way. He speaks directly to the pastors, or elders, of the churches concerning their role (5:1–4). But the larger theme that permeates today's reading is the issue of suffering.

APPLICATION

The word *suffering* appears at least eleven times in today's passage in some form. It was a major part of the believers' lives in the first century, and it continues to be part of our lives today as we deal with the collateral damage caused by sin. How should we handle this reality?

We should learn to expect it. "Think it not strange" (4:12). To live for Christ in a broken world is to swim upstream. The world around us, the devil beneath us, and the flesh within us will cause grief and pain. Often, suffering is part of "the will of God" (4:19) for believers.

We shouldn't fear it. "Be not afraid…neither be troubled" (3:14). God holds you in the palm of His hand and won't let go. He is sovereign and in control of your circumstances. He will only allow you to endure that which He already intends and is able to use for your good.

We should be joyful in it. "Be glad also with exceeding joy" (4:13). You have much to smile about, even in suffering. You have a Saviour who loves you, gave His life for you, and is preparing a home in Heaven for you to enjoy. And your suffering identifies you with Him as one of the "partakers of Christ's sufferings."

We should allow God to use it. "Let him glorify God" (4:16). When you testify of the Lord's goodness when things go well, people expect it. But when you testify of His goodness in the midst of suffering, people take notice. Your poise, grace, and strength while suffering speak volumes about the power of God in your life.

We should trust God during it. "Commit the keeping of their souls to him" (4:19). He is truly a "faithful Creator." We can trust Him to grant us the needed strength and to use our suffering for our good and the advancement of His purposes. He declares from the very beginning how the end will turn out (Isaiah 46:10), and He knows what He's doing.

Dear Lord, I'm thankful that I can trust You during suffering. Long before I ever faced any suffering, You went to the cross of Calvary to endure the greatest suffering ever experienced on my behalf. So may I never question or resent You when You allow suffering in my life. May I trust You, rejoice in You, and glorify You. Please grant me the strength to do so.

"Beloved, think it not strange concerning the fiery trial which is to try you, as though some strange thing happened unto you: But rejoice, inasmuch as ye are partakers of Christ's sufferings; that, when his glory shall be revealed, ye may be glad also with exceeding joy."

1 Peter 4:12–13

DAY 80

2 PETER 1–3

Peter's Letter to Believers He Hoped Would Flourish

OVERVIEW

Peter's second letter is to the same audience as his first, mostly Gentile believers in a region known today as Turkey. This letter is his last as he anticipates his coming martyrdom (1:14–15). Historians believe Peter wrote this letter from a Roman prison shortly before he was crucified upside down.

Three themes emerge from the letter's three chapters, involving three different groups. Chapter 1 is focused on the believers and their spiritual growth. God's desire is that we know Him increasingly and bear the fruit of maturity. Chapter 2 focuses on false prophets, whose destructive influence threatens the believers and, if followed, will take them backwards in their faith. Chapter 3 focuses on defending the return of Christ against scoffers who denied the promise of our Lord's return.

APPLICATION

Knowing God—it's what the Bible is all about. It's why Christ came to earth and went to the cross. And it's the most important matter in life.

Coming to know God makes us a Christian. *Growing* in our knowledge of Him is what fuels our development as Christians. By "knowledge of Him," I don't mean knowledge *about* Him, but rather getting to know Him personally through experience, like a spouse knows his or her mate better over the years.

Knowing God is where 2 Peter begins (1:2–3) and where it ends (3:18). The opening verses beautifully explain that knowing God is the means by which we receive four important spiritual commodities: grace, peace, life, and godliness.

- Grace: This is the favor of God we receive even though we don't deserve it. As we deepen our experience with Him through Bible study, prayer, obedience, and Spirit-led living, we open up the connection for greater amounts of His grace to flow our way.

- Peace: The better we know God, the more peace we'll possess. We won't panic, stress, or worry, because we know the One who holds tomorrow. And, as the songwriter said, we know He holds our hand. No need to fear the storm if the Master is on board our vessel.
- Life: The Christian life is impossible to live successfully without God's enabling. As we know Him more, we receive everything we need in order to live with the right words, thoughts, attitudes, and actions.
- Godliness: Becoming more like God and His Son, Jesus Christ, requires that we know Him better. We tend to mimic those we spend time with and know best. Know Him more and you'll reflect Him more.

I trust you already know God. But I suspect you long to know Him better. This is His desire too. It's a standing invitation—you can know Him as deeply as you wish. What a privilege!

Lord God, thank You for giving me "all things that pertain unto life and godliness." You have given me so much, starting with Your Son and continuing with Your daily supply of grace and mercy. Great is Your faithfulness! Empower me to live the life You have saved me to live—spiritually vibrant, fruitful, mature, and godly. I know I cannot do it on my own, so I ask for Your enabling.

"According as his divine power hath given unto us all things that pertain unto life and godliness, through the knowledge of him that hath called us to glory and virtue:"

2 Peter 1:3

DAY 81

1 JOHN 1–3

Faith in the Son, Obedience to the Father, Love for the Brethren

OVERVIEW

John was, at the writing of this letter, the last of the living apostles. Historians tell us he had an evangelistic ministry and a role as overseer throughout the churches in Asia Minor. This letter is an authoritative message to John's children in the faith, designed to strengthen them against false teaching such as Gnosticism, which was beginning to emerge toward the end of the first century. John seeks to provide marks for authentic Christianity to prevent the recipients of the letter from swallowing a counterfeit faith.

John wrote that the distinguishing marks of believers would include these characteristics: 1) *Faith* in the Christ the apostles preached (as opposed to a counterfeit version describing Him as less than fully God; 2) *Obedience* to the Father; and 3) *Love* for one's brethren in the faith.

One quick word of clarification. John is *not* saying (in verses such as 3:6), "If you sin, you're not saved." Both 1:8–9 and 2:1 dispel this idea. He is expressing that a true believer's life should not be defined by sin but by the overcoming of it.

APPLICATION

What did John mean by the command, "Love not the world" (2:15)? The term *world,* translated from the Greek *kosmos,* takes on three different connotations in the New Testament, depending on its use and context. It can refer to:

- The world that God created, as in the Earth, solar system, universe, etc.
- The world of people, as in, everyone. "God so loved the world" (John 3:16).
- The world, as in, the system of culture and kingdoms, driven and defined by mankind's fallen nature, which has been corrupted by the effects of sin and which stands in temporary opposition to God and His authority.

It is clearly this third definition of the *world*, to which John refers, when he says, "Love not the world, neither the things that are in the world." John makes it plain—you can either love the world or you can love God. But you can't love both, because you'll have to let go of one to embrace the other. He learned this from Jesus (Matthew 6:24).

John goes on to define how exactly the world allures believers (2:16):

- "The lust of the flesh"—*pleasures.* These are the things our body craves but God has forbidden, including drugs, sexual immorality, and other cheap thrills.
- "The lust of the eyes"—*possessions.* These are the things our eyes notice and we desire to the point of discontent and covetousness.
- "The pride of life"—*power.* This is the obsession with increasing our accomplishments or authority.

As you consider these three categories of worldly interests, can you see how easy it is to get drawn in, making them our pursuit, our focus, our *love*? Let's be reminded today that these things leave us unsatisfied, because we were created for more. We were created for another world and designed to be fulfilled only by God Himself, which is why loving and pursuing Him is the only choice worth making.

Heavenly Father, I confess to You that the things of this world often catch my eye. And when they do, I'm tempted to foolishly chase them. Please forgive me for pursuing other things to the neglect of pursuing You. I do love You. And I long to love You more fully. I want to go on record right now that You are my heart's desire, and I ask for Your help as I make You my life's one true pursuit.

"Love not the world, neither the things that are in the world. If any man love the world, the love of the Father is not in him."

1 John 2:15

DAY 82

1 JOHN 4–5

Overcoming the World and Loving God

OVERVIEW

Similar themes continue from the first half of John's letter to the closing half. The apostle is concerned that the believers not be swept off course from the simple, saving message of Jesus Christ. Their role as believers is to love God, keep His commandments, love one another, and allow His truth to define their lives.

APPLICATION

John paints the picture of opposing forces in this universe. On one side, the world opposes God and denies the truth of His Son. While on the other side, true believers love God and root their lives in His Son.

It appears that some Christians think they can follow God *while* walking in lockstep with the culture of this world. But it's impossible—an exercise in futility.

We need discernment. John said, "Believe not every spirit…many false prophets are gone out into the world" (4:1). How true John's words are today!

The voices of numerous spirits speak into our lives through the internet, television, the music industry, university classrooms, social media, and more.

- The spirit of materialism (the pursuit of stuff)
- The spirit of sexual immorality (forget God's rules of moral purity)
- The spirit of narcissism (it's all about me)
- The spirit of secularism (man's mind rules supreme)
- The spirit of plurality and polytheism (all faiths are the same)
- The spirit of relativism (there's no fixed right and wrong)
- The spirit of skepticism (God is not real)

All of these offer false and destructive philosophies, and gullible Christians must stop swallowing the lies preached by the prophets of this world. They're false. They're empty, and following them leads to tragedy. Why follow a broken system that's piloted by misguided people and bound for destruction?

"Greater is he that is in you, than he that is in the world" (4:4). There is a great God who sent His Son, who died on a cross for you, who rose from the grave, and who invites you into a relationship with Him, in which He will guide you into a life of abundance, joy, and eternity. He is "in you." And you're going to follow yesterday's internet sensation instead? You're going to get your advice on life's issues from a pop singer?

While the world marches toward Hell in rejection of Christ, John calls God's children to break rank and instead follow God and His truth. Our task is not to follow the world, but rather to overcome the world (4:4, 5:4) and follow Christ.

"The Son of God is come, and hath given us an understanding, that we may know him that is true" (5:20). Let's determine to be believers of understanding who know God increasingly and daily align our lives with His truth.

Lord God, please grant me guidance that I might walk in your truth and avoid the errors being peddled by this broken world in which I am living. Protect me from the lies and tactics of the enemy, who is bent on destroying me. Thank you for living in me, by way of the Holy Spirit. Please use your Word and your Spirit to lead me in truth, every step of the way. And help me take others along with me.

"Ye are of God, little children, and have overcome them: because greater is he that is in you, than he that is in the world."

1 John 4:4

DAY 83

2 JOHN, 3 JOHN, JUDE

Three Little-but-Powerful Letters from the First Century

OVERVIEW

Second John was written for the same purpose as 1 John—to strengthen the believers' stance in truth, obedience, and love for Christ and others. Second John was, however, written to a more specific audience. While 1 John was written to believers in a region, 2 John was delivered to a particular congregation that met in a woman's house.

Third John is the most personal of the apostle's letters. It's addressed to a believer named Gaius, whose Christian hospitality John commends. In the letter, John identifies one who opposes him and his colleagues, named Diotrephes, who apparently usurped leadership in a congregation to serve his own agenda. This letter is delivered by a faithful helper named Demetrius.

Jude was the brother of James (whose letter we read just a week ago) and another one of the half-brothers of Jesus Christ. His letter was written earlier than John's letters, probably around A.D. 65–70. He wrote to believers who were suffering persecution (as James and Peter did) and who were susceptible to false teaching (as John did). In light of both of these realities, he challenged them to fight ("contend" v. 3) for the truths ("the faith") they had been entrusted.

APPLICATION

As John the apostle neared the end of his life, he wrote to the believers about what was most important. Approaching one's departure helps narrow down what to transfer to those receiving the baton. And for John, this was easy—it was all about Jesus Christ.

The zenith of all doctrine is Jesus Christ. And there were people in John's day—as there are in ours—who wanted Christians to tone down their beliefs about Jesus. These forces don't ask believers to reject Jesus, they simply want us to agree that Jesus is one of many gods or religious leaders, all equal in their value or deity.

But a Christian cannot say that Jesus is just like Buddha, Muhammed, or Confucius. Because the very essence of being a Christian is to believe in Christ—to believe what the Bible says about Him (2 John 9).

Here's what we believe about Jesus: He is the preexistent, eternal Son of God, co-equal with God as Creator and Sovereign Lord. He was born of a virgin, lived a sinless life, performed miracles, died as God's only acceptable substitute for sinners, was buried, and rose from the grave three days later. He ascended to Heaven where He continues to reign with the Father. And the only way to have a relationship with God and an eternal home in Heaven is to receive Him personally as Saviour, placing our trust in Him alone for the forgiveness of our sin.

Friend, if that's not what you believe about Jesus, you're not a Christian. That's not my opinion. That's Jesus' (John 14:6) and John's (John 20:31) and Paul's (Romans 5:10) and Peter's (Acts 4:12) and every other biblical writer's we have read over the past eighty-two days.

Times change, but this doesn't. Isn't that comforting and reassuring? Jesus is God. What a doctrine. What a Saviour!

Lord Jesus, I praise You for who You are. You are God alone. You have chosen to love and forgive and accept and bless me. I could never thank You enough. May I never be ashamed of You. May I speak of You to others with boldness, compassion, and clarity. And may I walk with You, enjoying Your presence.

"Whosoever transgresseth, and abideth not in the doctrine of Christ, hath not God. He that abideth in the doctrine of Christ, he hath both the Father and the Son."

2 John 9

DAY 84

REVELATION 1–3

A Message from Jesus for Seven Churches

OVERVIEW

The word *revelation* means "an uncovering" or "an unveiling." And verse 1 of this book says that it's the revelation "of Jesus Christ." So this book's intent is to reveal to us things about Jesus Christ—specifically His authoritative rule over history and nations, and His triumphant return at the end of the age.

This revelation was given by an angel to the apostle John (1:1). This is John's last book, and he writes it from the island of Patmos where he had been exiled as a prisoner as a result of preaching the gospel (1:9). The book is sent to seven specific churches mentioned in chapters 2–3, likely the ones John had ministered to before his exile.

After an introduction to the book (chapter 1) and a specific message for each of the seven churches (chapters 2–3), the remaining nineteen chapters are entirely prophetic in nature. They forecast days that have yet to occur on God's timetable. What an encouragement to these struggling churches that were suffering under the hands of brutal emperors to learn that Jesus Christ rules from the throne of Heaven, exercising His authority over the affairs of men and nations. He will one day bring every evil act to final justice and welcome His children home to eternal joy.

APPLICATION

As Jesus addresses the seven churches, He starts with Ephesus (2:1). That's significant, since Ephesus was where John spent most of his time during the latter half of his ministry.

Jesus has some commendations for the believers in Ephesus (2:2–3). They had labored diligently and patiently. They had rejected evil deceivers. They had been faithful. But Jesus goes on to say, "Nevertheless I have somewhat against thee…" (2:4). What could Jesus possibly find to correct?

"Thou hast left thy first love." Ouch. They had fallen out of love with Him. The devotion and affection they had for Jesus had diminished. This can happen to us, too, can't it? We're laboring hard. We're being faithful. But while we have been working, we have forgotten *who* we are working for and *why* we are doing it. We are just going through motions.

Losing our first love usually involves getting "too busy" for quiet time with God. It often involves going from one project to the next, working to keep all of life's plates spinning. It's miserable.

What do we do when our passion for and excitement over Jesus needs re-igniting? He said to the Ephesians, "Remember therefore from whence thou art fallen, and repent, and do the first works" (2:5). In other words, hit a reset button. Carve out some quiet time with Jesus. Tell Him you're sorry, and put into place some disciplines to daily feed the fire and fan the flames of your love for Him. He is easy to love, if we would just stay near.

Lord Jesus, I confess to You that I need to love You more. I need to think of You more. I need to pursue You more. I need to praise You and speak to You and listen to You more. Please forgive me for having left my first love for You. I repent. Please draw near to me as I draw near to You. I love You, Lord.

"Nevertheless I have somewhat against thee, because thou hast left thy first love. Remember therefore from whence thou art fallen, and repent, and do the first works; or else I will come unto thee quickly, and will remove thy candlestick out of his place, except thou repent."

Revelation 2:4–5

DAY 85

REVELATION 4–6

God's Glory in Heaven; God's Judgment on Earth

OVERVIEW

In 4:1, John is summoned to "come up hither," which means, in this vision, to enter Heaven and receive a glimpse of what we believers will experience upon our eventual arrival. The angel says that John will be shown "things which must be hereafter," referring to events mapped out on God's timetable to follow the church age in which we are now living.

Chapters 4–5 describe the grand and glorious throne room in Heaven, where the Lord receives the praise of twenty-four elders (who represent Old Testament saints and New Testament believers), four beasts (an exalted order of angels), and an incalculable number of additional angels, creatures, and redeemed people—from every spectrum of creation. In chapter 5 we see that the "Lamb," the Lord Jesus, is also an object of this praise. He is the only one able to open the book containing the prophecies that compose the remaining pages of the Revelation.

This book is opened by the breaking of seven seals. Six of these seals are opened in chapter 6, revealing the traumatic events that will take place during the seven-year Tribulation period. This is the beginning of a final judgment to be executed on the earth and its inhabitants. As indicated by John's being called up into Heaven at the beginning of chapter 4, those who know the Lord will have already been removed from the earth (the Rapture) before this Tribulation period begins.

APPLICATION

So often we forget that the world does not revolve around ourselves. We tend to focus on our concerns, our relationships, our interests, and our immediate wants and needs. But the reality is that we are part of something much larger. The scene in Heaven reminds us of this.

God doesn't exist for our benefit. We exist for Him. According to 4:11, all creation exists for His pleasure. All of creation is designed to give Him the glory He's worthy of and to advance the eternal purposes that are rooted in His wisdom, goodness, and sovereignty.

Life isn't about the here and now; it's about eternity. It's not about me; it's about God. I'm privileged to be part of His grand plan and a recipient of His grace. My life is designed to be wrapped up in Him and centered around Him, not the other way around. Only then will I find the satisfaction and identity and purpose I have been looking for.

The glimpses we get into Heaven in the book of Revelation emphasize some important truths that should guide how we live today: Life is larger than our concerns. Eternity is longer than our lives. And God is far greater than anything and everything that He has created.

Lord, as I consider Your throne in Heaven, I acknowledge Your great glory and Your extraordinary holiness. You are the Sovereign King over all of the universe, and I gladly recognize Your Lordship over my life. I look forward to arriving in Heaven and enjoying eternity with You. May I worship and serve and honor You today, in preparation for that day.

"The four and twenty elders fall down before him that sat on the throne, and worship him that liveth for ever and ever, and cast their crowns before the throne, saying, Thou art worthy, O Lord, to receive glory and honour and power: for thou hast created all things, and for thy pleasure they are and were created."

Revelation 4:10–11

DAY 86

REVELATION 7–9

The Seventh Seal of God's Judgment Is Opened

OVERVIEW

Jesus, the Lamb, continues to open the seals of judgment contained in Heaven's book. Just before the seventh seal is opened, a remnant of God's servants on earth, comprising 144,000 Jewish believers (who apparently came to faith in Christ after the Rapture) are "sealed" to be protected from the increasing judgments to come.

As the seventh seal is opened, seven angels are released with seven trumpets. With the sounding of each of their trumpets, there's a ratcheting up of God's wrath on earth's inhabitants. After numerous cataclysmic phenomena and the attack of torturous locusts, a full one-third of the world's population dies. In spite of all this, mankind's idolatry and rejection of God continues during this Tribulation period.

APPLICATION

There are two very different scenes depicted in today's reading: one in Heaven (chapter 7) and the other on earth (chapters 8–9). The scene in Heaven involves joy and praise, while the scene on earth involves suffering and destruction. These scenes provide a clear contrast to life with God compared to life without Him. Heaven is defined by God's presence; by the time these prophesies are fulfilled, earth is nearly devoid of His presence, inhabited almost entirely by those who reject and oppose Him.

Consider Heaven: There is an innumerable number (7:9) of people. Multiplied millions have received Christ through the ages. This multitude is multi-cultural, comprising those from "all nations, and kindreds, and people, and tongues." This beautiful, multi-ethnic choir singing praise to God reminds us to be gracious toward all and grateful for the work of missionaries around the world. The beginning of their song is "Salvation" (7:10), because they have been washed by the blood of the

Lamb (7:14), whom they serve day and night. There is no more hunger, thirst, or tears (7:16–17).

Consider earth: Mankind begins to realize that this cataclysmic judgment is from God. And in spite of the famine, destruction, and death, men in their stubborn rebellion will not repent. They "worship devils, and idols of gold, and silver, and brass, and stone, and of wood: which neither can see, nor hear, nor walk: Neither repented they of their murders, nor of their sorceries, nor of their fornication, nor of their thefts" (9:20–21). Mankind is so stubborn in his rejection of God that he would rather worship statues while continuing to experience judgment than repent and humble himself before God. This rejection seals his fate of eternal suffering.

How should we respond to these coming realities? We should rejoice over the glory that awaits us, which we will enjoy only because of the grace of God. And we should be burdened for those who do not know God, getting the gospel to as many as we can before it's eternally too late.

Heavenly Father, I look forward to my arrival in Heaven and joining that choir in praise to You. Thank You for making my entrance possible through the blood of Your precious Son. Blessing, glory, wisdom, thanksgiving, honor, power, and might belong to You—for ever and ever.

"After this I beheld, and, lo, a great multitude, which no man could number, of all nations, and kindreds, and people, and tongues, stood before the throne, and before the Lamb, clothed with white robes, and palms in their hands; And cried with a loud voice, saying, Salvation to our God which sitteth upon the throne, and unto the Lamb."

Revelation 7:9–10

DAY 87

REVELATION 10–12

Tribulation Judgments Reach Their Midway Point

OVERVIEW

Chapter 10 through chapter 11:14 appear to be an interlude between the sixth and seventh angel. During this interlude, another angel demonstrates God's ultimate authority by planting one foot on a continent and another foot in an ocean, overseeing the judgments. We are also introduced to two witnesses (possibly Moses and Elijah in resurrected form) who preach God's judgment, inviting people to repent and turn to God. The world rejoices when "the beast" (Antichrist) executes them but is surprised when they rise from the dead after three days and ascend to Heaven.

The remainder of chapters 11–12 describes the events of the seventh angel's trumpet sound. This signals the second half of the tribulation, when the Antichrist will break his peace treaty with Israel and launch persecution upon her people, many of whom have by this time embraced the message of Jesus Christ. In chapter 12, the woman symbolizes Israel, and the dragon symbolizes Satan. While the dragon seeks to destroy the woman, she is miraculously preserved by God, in spite of persecution.

APPLICATION

The sounding of the seventh trumpet judgment is a sort of final call, an announcement that things are in motion on an unalterable course, over which God has total control. The temporary influence of the devil and his forces (Ephesians 6:12), which has caused damage for centuries, is about to end. The thrones of this world are about to be turned back to the control of their rightful Owner. You can sense the excitement of the redeemed and the angels in Heaven (11:15).

History records countless suffering, faithful saints who long for God to bring justice to this broken world. They include the psalmist, who observes the prosperity of the wicked; the apostle, who is executed for preaching the gospel; the martyr of the Reformation, burned at the stake; the Christian in today's communist or Islamic country, persecuted for his or her faith; and the believer who suffered abuse or was the innocent victim of someone else's sin.

The seventh trumpet acknowledges all of these people and more. Most supremely, this trumpet will make right the greatest miscarriage of justice the world has ever known, the crucifixion of the Son of God on a cross at Calvary. This trumpet signals the setting in motion of every right that every wrong demands.

Don't get discouraged over the unsolved problems and unanswered questions that so characterize today's world. God's timetable continues to move toward its final judgment hour. And there's a world coming that'll be totally worth the wait.

Lord God, I bow my heart to You now, in anticipation of the worship that I'll participate in for all eternity. I rejoice to consider that Your plan is already underway to fully repossess the kingdoms of this world. Foolish dictators and silly politicians think they're in charge today, but all their thrones and palaces and parliaments and congresses belong to You. And You will rule over it all in goodness, wisdom, and love. Thank You for making me part of Your great and eternal Kingdom.

"And the seventh angel sounded; and there were great voices in heaven, saying, The kingdoms of this world are become the kingdoms of our Lord, and of his Christ; and he shall reign for ever and ever."

Revelation 11:15

DAY 88

REVELATION 13–15

Two Evil Beasts, One Almighty Lamb, and a Faithful Remnant

OVERVIEW

Two evil personalities, both symbolically referred to as "beasts" in chapter 13, lead the world during this period. The first beast, the Antichrist, is a political and military leader. Halfway through the tribulation he appears to die and rise again, prompting the worship of the world's population. The second beast, the False Prophet, is a religious leader. After uniting the world's apostate religions, he will direct people's worship toward the Antichrist. Both of these leaders are empowered by the devil (the dragon).

These demonic leaders are contrasted by the Lamb who, though in Heaven at that time, has His loyal followers on earth, the 144,000 Jewish evangelists. There are also others who follow Jesus, though their persecution under the Antichrist and False Prophet will be severe.

As chapter 15 closes, we are introduced to yet seven more angels, who in the next phase in the seventh trumpet judgment, each carry a vial (bowl) filled with God's wrath, which will shortly be poured out on earth, once again ratcheting up the severity of God's judgment.

APPLICATION

At the time of the Rapture, which is the next prophetic event on God's current timetable, all believers will be immediately caught up to Heaven. Thankfully, that means you and I won't be around for the Tribulation.

There will, however, be many who come to faith in Christ during the Tribulation, and these believers—our spiritual brothers and sisters—will suffer through this awful time. But they will be loyal (14:4). They will refuse the mark of the beast, a mandated stamp required to conduct business in the Antichrist's world economy. They will suffer persecution and many will be killed. But they are overcomers! What do we know about them?

- They preach the gospel, seeking to turn unbelievers from faith in the Antichrist to faith in the one true Christ. Their message is like the angel's: "Fear God, and give glory to him; for the hour of his judgment is come: and worship him" (14:7).
- They patiently endure (14:12). Even though the entire population of the world is rallying in great unity behind the Antichrist and in opposition to the God of Creation, these faithful few maintain their obedience to the Lord.
- They keep faith in Jesus (14:12). They keep depending on Him and waiting for His ultimate deliverance. I imagine they constantly pray, review the promises found in His Word, sing, and encourage one another.

If they will be faithful then, we can be faithful now! Remain pure. Preach the gospel. Endure. Keep believing. Though these believers haven't yet been through their test, they still are our example. Let's follow their lead.

Lord Jesus, Lamb of God, I praise You for Your sovereign authority over this world, both now and during the Tribulation and for all eternity. The challenges I face today do not compare to the horrors my brothers and sisters will endure during the Tribulation. And You will give them the strength and grace to be faithful. Please grant me that same strength and grace. Help me be a faithful witness for You today.

"Here is the patience of the saints: here are they that keep the commandments of God, and the faith of Jesus."

Revelation 14:12

DAY 89

REVELATION 16–18

Seven Vials of Wrath Poured Out on Babylon

OVERVIEW

As part of the seventh trumpet judgment, seven vials containing God's wrath are poured out on the earth's inhabitants. Disease will plague mankind, water sources will be turned to blood, scorching heat, drought, and darkness will be unleashed. Instead of repenting, the world's armies will assemble for battle, first against the Jewish nation and Christ's followers and finally (in chapter 19), against God Himself.

Chapter 17 introduces us to the "great whore," which represents the false, idolatrous, one-world organized religion. And while the whore, the dragon, and the beasts work in tandem, taking out their anger on God's people, God's judgment upon their population continues.

The Antichrist's political capitol, Babylon, known during the first half of the Tribulation as a mighty economic and political center of power, will fall under God's judgment (this is not necessarily the historical or geographical Babylon, but symbolic of the Antichrist's kingdom). World political and business leaders (kings, merchants, shipmasters) will grieve over Babylon's fall. But Heaven will rejoice, as justice is carried out for the deaths of millions of God's children throughout the ages.

APPLICATION

If you were asked to summarize in one statement the reigns of Caesar Augustus, Napoleon Bonaparte, Alexander the Great, Adolf Hitler, and the coming Antichrist, how would you do it? Here's a suggestion: "And the Lamb shall overcome them."

Empires rise and fall. World leaders ascend to power. Military forces march forward. These are frightening to behold. But not even the strongest earthly military with the most elite national defense comes close to matching the might, authority, and awesome power of our great God. He is "King of kings and Lord of lords." He takes orders from no one. He needs no assistance in accomplishing His will, and He needs no consultation on battle strategy.

This is what the Tribulation events reveal about our Saviour, Jesus Christ, in 17:14. But notice what's revealed to John next, in that very same verse: "and they that are with him are called, and chosen, and faithful."

Called. Chosen. Faithful. That's how Revelation describes those who follow the Lamb. That's you, if you have received Christ as Saviour.

These aren't goals you should live up to but rather facts about you. You are *called*—God has a purpose and plan for your life. You are *chosen*—He has known you since before you existed and has fit you into His design for the ages. You are *faithful*—if you're an authentic believer, God says you're going to make it to the finish line, so accept it by faith. That doesn't mean you won't stumble along the way. But you'll finish.

Lift your chin, square your shoulders back, and put one foot in front of the other—you're with the Lamb. And He overcomes!

Lord Jesus, I praise You for Your great power and authority to overcome. You overcame temptation during Your earthly ministry. You overcame death when You rose from the grave. You overcame my sin when You saved my soul. And one day You'll overcome one final and everlasting time, to end the ages and launch us into an eternity, when You will reign and we will enjoy Your glory and fellowship. Amen!

"These shall make war with the Lamb, and the Lamb shall overcome them: for he is Lord of lords, and King of kings: and they that are with him are called, and chosen, and faithful."

Revelation 17:14

DAY 90

REVELATION 19–22

As the Tribulation Ends, the Millennial Reign Begins, Followed by Eternal Glory

OVERVIEW

We learn in chapter 19 that there are "much people" (v. 1) in Heaven praising God. The King of Kings and Lord of Lords (v. 16) gathers His armies (v. 14) for the final execution of His wrath upon the beast and the armies of the world, which have gathered at Armageddon. They prove to be no match for our conquering Lord.

Chapter 20 describes the one-thousand year reign of Jesus Christ on the earth, where His children preside over a blessed global kingdom while the devil is bound in a bottomless pit (vv. 1–3). Satan is freed for a brief moment at the end of this millennial kingdom when he rallies deceived armies against the Lord one final time. This battle is even more swift than Armageddon, as fire devours them before they even have the opportunity to attack. After this, the Great White Throne judgment occurs, where those who have opposed God and rejected His Son will be sentenced to the lake of fire.

Chapters 21–22 explain that the earth will be completely remade, with the curse of sin removed. A glorious, breathtakingly beautiful new Heaven will also descend from above, where those who followed God from all ages will enjoy Him and glorify Him forever.

APPLICATION

Because we lead physical lives on earthly soil, we often forget that we were made for more. We consider eighty or ninety years as "a good, long life." But this is merely the warm-up act—the dress rehearsal. If we really knew what *that* life will be in its fullness, we would probably see this life differently.

We are too tied up with issues related to *this* life. We think over, talk about, and prepare for the life that's to come far too little. That's why Paul said, "Set your affection on things above, not on things on the earth" (Colossians 3:2).

I suggest you enjoy the moments of this life and the good things God extends to you. But I caution you to avoid worshiping them. Houses, cars, vacations, sports, hobbies, academic degrees, career accomplishments—they're all gracious gifts from a generous God, and we should enjoy them. But we should do so acknowledging that there's a greater, longer, more significant life to come.

"God himself shall be with them" (21:3). The God no man has ever fully seen since the Garden of Eden will be with us. After thousands of years of human history, because of the cross of Calvary, we will be reunited at last.

The love, thrill , satisfaction, glory and fulfillment of being with Him will surpass all past experiences. It will cause every earthly item we were ever tempted to idolize to fade into the distant background. Those things will seem like nothing compared to what we'll experience in Heaven with our good and great God.

Dear God, I'm amazed when I consider Your greatness, power and authority. I'm amazed when I consider Your redemption of mankind. I'm amazed when I consider that I'm involved in all of this as Your child, follower, and servant. You're in Heaven even now, and I'll be there too, one day. What a joy. Thank You for making it possible.

"...Behold, the tabernacle of God is with men, and he will dwell with them, and they shall be his people, and God himself shall be with them, and be their God. And God shall wipe away all tears from their eyes; and there shall be no more death, neither sorrow, nor crying, neither shall there be any more pain: for the former things are passed away."

Revelation 21:3–4

· BIBLIOGRAPHY ·

Chapell, Bryan. *Praying Backwards: Transform Your Prayer Life by Beginning in Jesus' Name.* Grand Rapids, MI: Baker Books, 2005.

Chappell, Stephen. *Lessons from the Road: A Study from the Gospel of Mark.* Lancaster, CA: Striving Together Publications, 2015.

Phillips, John. *Exploring Colossians & Philemon: An Expository Commentary.* Grand Rapids, MI: Kregel Publications, 2002.

Phillips, John. *Exploring People of the Bible: Exploring People of the New Testament.* Grand Rapids, MI: Kregel Publications, 2007.

MacArthur, John. *The Macarthur New Testament Commentary.* Chicago, IL: Moody Publishers, 2015.

Wiersbe, Warren. *Be Diligent.* Colorado Springs, CO: David C. Cook, 1987.

· ABOUT THE AUTHOR ·

Tim Christoson is the pastor of Bible Baptist Church in Howell, Michigan. He and his wife, Nicole, have four children and have been serving the Lord in pastoral ministry together since their marriage in 1997. He finds great joy in serving the Lord and in seeing people develop in their faith, through the ministry of the local church.

OTHER DEVOTIONAL BOOKS WE THINK YOU WILL LOVE...

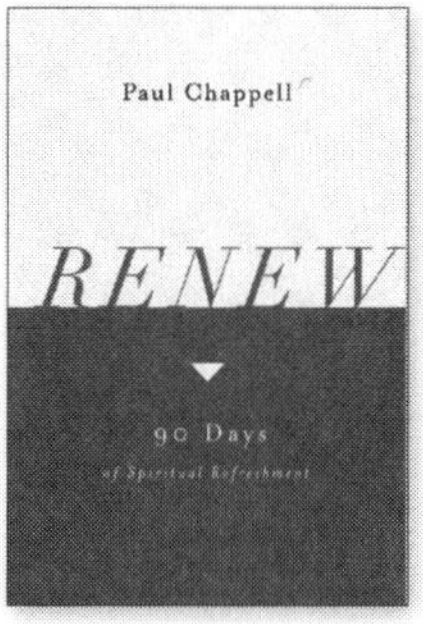

Renew By Paul Chappell

90 Days of Spiritual Refreshment

This ninety-day devotional guide will encourage you to seek God's face and renew your heart in His Word. Each devotion includes a Scripture passage and provides an encouraging or admonishing truth regarding your walk with the Lord.

Time Out for Parents By Paul Chappell

90 Days of Biblical Encouragement

The ninety devotions in this book are written to encourage parents to seek God's wisdom as they raise their children for Him. At the close of each devotion is a single actionable thought given as "Today's Parenting Principle."

Disciple By Paul Chappell

Daily Truths from the Gospel of Luke for Followers of Jesus

Each daily reading in Disciple will take you on a journey through the Gospel of Luke and the chronological account of the life of Christ. As these brief devotions draw you closer to the Lord, you'll be challenged and encouraged to follow Jesus more closely and to walk with Him each day.

OTHER DEVOTIONAL BOOKS WE THINK YOU WILL LOVE...

Trust and Obey By Paul Chappell

365 Devotions to Encourage Your Walk of Faith

Paul Chappell's Trust and Obey devotional will encourage your spiritual growth. The readings conclude with a solid takeaway principle which you can apply to your life immediately. You'll be challenged and encouraged to follow Jesus more closely and to walk with Him in practical ways throughout each day.

A Daily Word By Paul Chappell

366 Scriptural Devotions for Growing Christians

Designed to complement your daily devotional walk with the Lord, this book from Dr. Paul Chappell features 366 daily devotional thoughts to strengthen and encourage your spiritual life. Each devotion features a one-year Bible reading selection.

Revival Today By John Goetsch & Nathan Birt

365 Challenging Devotions from Revival History

Each devotion in this book is written to encourage you that revival is still possible today. Each daily reading describes an event or individual from the past that God has used to bring revival.

OTHER BOOKS WE THINK YOU WILL LOVE...

Outsiders By Paul Chappell

15 Leaders Who Followed Christ and Changed the World

Discover fifteen leaders from history who followed Christ and changed the world. Their testimonies will stir your faith, strengthen your commitment, and renew your dedication to Christ.

Are We There Yet? By Paul & Terrie Chappell

Marriage—The Perfect Journey for Imperfect Couples

This book is for every couple at any stage of the marriage journey. It will help reveal a God-given perspective that can change and strengthen your marriage. A companion guide is sold separately.

Making Home Work in a Broken Society

By Paul Chappell

Bible Principles for Raising Children and Building Families

God has entrusted you, as a parent, to care for and raise your children for Him—but it's not easy. Discover what it means to invest in your children and how you can bring them up in the nurture and admonition of the Lord.

STRIVINGTOGETHER.COM

ALSO AVAILABLE AS EBOOKS